GROW
TOGETHER NOW

VOLUME 2

- ✻ HUMILITY
- ✻ KINDNESS
- ✻ COOPERATION

Group resources really work!

This Group resource incorporates our R.E.A.L. approach to ministry. It reinforces a growing friendship with Jesus, encourages long-term learning, and results in life transformation, because it's

Relational
Learner-to-learner interaction enhances learning and builds Christian friendships.

Experiential
What learners experience through discussion and action sticks with them up to 9 times longer than what they simply hear or read.

Applicable
The aim of Christian education is to equip learners to be both hearers and doers of God's Word.

Learner-based
Learners understand and retain more when the learning process takes into consideration how they learn best.

TOGETHER NOW

Grow Together Now, Volume 2
Copyright © 2017 Group Publishing, Inc./0000 0001 0362 4853

Visit our website: **group.com**

CREDITS
Executive Editor: Jody Brolsma
Content Editor: Mike Nappa
Art Director: Veronica Preston
Designer: Andy Towler
Media Production Supervisor/Producer:
Illustrators: Paige Billin-Frye, Dana Regan, Pamela Johnson, Drew Krevi, Ronnie Rooney

ISBN 978-1-4707-5111-1

Printed in the United States of America.

10 9 8 7 6 5 4 3 2 1   19 18 17

HOW TO USE
GROW TOGETHER NOW

Grow Together Now is rooted in Scripture and engages kids to grow to be like Jesus. Use these lessons to equip kids with the character qualities they need to each become the person God created them to be. These exciting, hands-on Bible lessons feature the three character qualities of humility, kindness, and cooperation. Kids will explore each character quality in memorable activities that reinforce God's foundational plan for a fruitful Christian life.

With these lessons, you'll introduce kids of all ages to:

- **Humility**—Seeing myself the way God sees me.

- **Kindness**—Treating others as beloved creations of God.

- **Cooperation**—Working together to accomplish a goal.

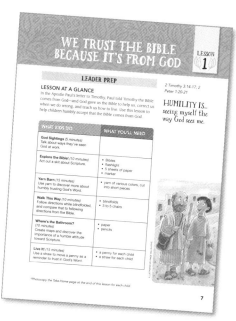

OVERVIEW CHART

This helpful chart gives you an overview of the lesson. Read "What Kids Do" first so you have the big picture of what will happen in your classroom with kids. Use the "What You'll Need" list to review and gather all the supplies you'll need for a great lesson.

DEVOTION FOR TEACHERS

Grow Together Now isn't just for children; it's for you, too!
Romans 8:29 says that God chose you "to become like his Son." With this devotion, let God speak to your heart and challenge you to grow in your friendship with him.

BIBLE FOUNDATION FOR TEACHERS

Each lesson includes an in-depth look into the related Bible passage. Allow God's Spirit to work in your heart and mind as you study the Scripture in preparation for your lesson.

THE LESSON

Research shows that people remember most of what they do but only a fraction of what they hear—which means that kids learn best by doing. Kids will act out skits, make things, create prayers, play games, do experiments, and actively participate in conversations to discover important biblical truths. Each lesson has the following features, plus more.

GOD SIGHTINGS

Talk about ways you've each seen God at work, and praise him!

BIBLE EXPLORATION

Dive into the Scripture with kids, and learn by doing a unique activity to drive home the point.

LIFE APPLICATION

Reinforce the message with an experience designed to help kids apply God's Word to their lives.

TAKE-HOME PAGE

Each week, kids will get six challenges on the Take-Home page. Encourage kids to choose at least one challenge to grow in character throughout the week. Let parents know that they can ask their children about the challenge and help when necessary.

TABLE OF CONTENTS

HUMILITY

LESSON 1
We Trust the Bible Because It's From God _____ 7
2 Timothy 3:14-17; 2 Peter 1:20-21: Scripture Is From God

LESSON 2
We Can be Humble—Just Like Jesus _____ 19
Luke 18:9-14: The Pharisee and the Tax Collector

LESSON 3
Humble Heroes Rely on God for Strength _____ 29
1 Samuel 17:1-50: David Defeats Goliath

LESSON 4
We're Content With What God Gives Us _____ 37
2 Samuel 12:1-6: Nathan Gives David a Message From God

KINDNESS

LESSON 5
We Love Others Because God Loves Us _____ 45
1 John 4:7-21: John Teaches About God's Love

LESSON 6
We Love as Jesus Loves _____ 53
Luke 23:44-49; 24:1-9: Jesus Dies for His Friends

LESSON 7
God Wants Us to be Kind to Others _____ 63
Ruth 1: Ruth Is Kind to Naomi

LESSON 8
We Show God's Kindness by Encouraging Each Other _____ 71
Genesis 37:3-36: Joseph Is Sold Into Slavery

LESSON 9
We Show God's Kindness to the World _____ 81
Matthew 5:13-16: Light of the World

COOPERATION

LESSON 10
We Can Get Along With Others _____ 91
2 Samuel 15: Absalom Rebels

LESSON 11
God Gives Us Gifts to Serve Others _____ 101
Acts 6:1-7: Seven Men Are Chosen to Serve

LESSON 12
We Work to Get Along With Our Families _____ 109
Genesis 13:1-18: Abram Is Generous to Lot

LESSON 13
When We Work Together, God Can Work Through Us _____ 119
1 Corinthians 12:12-27: The Importance of Everyone

WE TRUST THE BIBLE BECAUSE IT'S FROM GOD

LEADER PREP

LESSON AT A GLANCE

In the Apostle Paul's letter to Timothy, Paul told Timothy the Bible comes from God—and God gave us the Bible to help us, correct us when we do wrong, and teach us how to live. Use this lesson to help children humbly accept that the Bible comes from God.

2 Timothy 3:14-17;
2 Peter 1:20-21

HUMILITY IS...
seeing myself the way God sees me.

WHAT KIDS DO	WHAT YOU'LL NEED
God Sightings *(5 minutes)* Talk about ways they've seen God at work.	
Explore the Bible! *(10 minutes)* Act out a skit about Scripture.	• Bibles • flashlight • 5 sheets of paper • marker
Yarn Barn *(15 minutes)* Use yarn to discover more about humbly trusting God's Word.	• yarn of various colors, cut into short pieces
Walk This Way *(10 minutes)* Follow directions while blindfolded, and compare that to following directions from the Bible.	• blindfolds • 3 to 5 chairs
Where's the Bathroom? *(10 minutes)* Create maps, and discover the importance of a humble attitude toward Scripture.	• Bible • paper • pencils
Live It! *(15 minutes)* Use a straw to move a penny as a reminder to trust in God's Word.	• 1 penny per child • 1 straw per child

ILLUSTRATED BY PAIGE BILLIN-FRYE

*Photocopy the Take-Home page at the end of this lesson for each child.

DEVOTIONS FOR LEADERS:

HUMILITY

We live in an age of transient text—words that are here today and gone tomorrow in an information-rich society. Isn't it nice to know that God's Word never changes? And what a perfect reflection of God's love, unchanging and manifested in Jesus. If you don't already have a personal Bible-reading plan, consider developing one. While you're at it, encourage kids to take a Bible-reading adventure where they can spend time getting to know Jesus more fully!

BIBLE BACKGROUND FOR LEADERS

2 Timothy 3:14-17; 2 Peter 1:20-21: Scripture Is From God

IT'S ACCURATE

In 2 Timothy and 2 Peter, Jesus' apostles affirm the accuracy of Scripture as the Word inspired by God. Second Timothy is the last letter Paul wrote before he was put to death for his faith. Alone in prison, he wrote it to his young friend Timothy, who was a pastor of a church Paul had founded. Among other points in the letter, Paul gave Timothy advice about trusting the Bible—the Holy Scripture inspired by God.

IT'S INSPIRED BY GOD

Paul's term "inspired by God" assures us that God was involved in the writing of the Bible as he worked through human authors. That assurance helps us know that what we have in the Bible today is what God wants us to have. It tells us everything about him that he wants us to know. If we study it carefully and use it as our source for teaching, correcting, preparing, and equipping, we'll not only learn about God but also get to know God in a special and personal way.

IT INCLUDES THE NEW TESTAMENT

In 2 Timothy 3:14-17, Paul emphasizes the importance and reliability of God's Word. Timothy would've interpreted this to mean the Temple scrolls—Scripture he would've known as a child. Timothy understood that the Scriptures were meant to teach, correct, prepare, and equip; and Paul emphasized that Scripture is good for all things. Paul's reference to "all Scripture" applies to the whole of what we know as the Bible today.

ILLUSTRATED BY DANA REGAN

IT TELLS ABOUT JESUS

In 2 Peter, the Apostle Peter refutes the accusations of false teachers who insinuated that he and the other apostles had made up stories about Jesus and his power. After relating his own eyewitness accounts of Jesus' miracles, Peter turned to the prophets' witness to substantiate that Jesus was who he claimed to be. Peter put all prophecy and authorship of Bible texts into perspective: The writers of Scripture wrote only as inspired by God and guided by the Holy Spirit. Likely Peter was suggesting here that God wouldn't tolerate false stories about Jesus—accounts of his life could not have come from human imaginations any more than the prophets' claims came from their imaginations.

THE LESSON

GOD SIGHTINGS

Use the text below or substitute your own examples for this weekly lesson-starter activity.

Say: **James 1:17 in the Bible reminds us that "Whatever is good and perfect is a gift coming down to us from God our Father." That means the gift of a beautiful sunset is evidence of God. When your friend shares with you, that's God's kindness at work. When you smile at others or hold open a door, you're showing God's joy.**

It's important that we recognize and thank God for the ways we see him all around us and the ways he is at work in our lives. We call these God Sightings.

Ask: **How have you seen God at work this week? What evidence have you seen of God's creativity, joy, forgiveness, or goodness?**

Think about God's creation, ways people have encouraged you, and even ways God helped you make a difference for someone else.

As a group, share God Sightings. Then celebrate God's gifts in your lives with a prayer of thanksgiving.

✓ **Bibles**

✓ **flashlight**

✓ **5 sheets of paper**

✓ **marker**

✓ **photocopies of "The Bible Is the Best!" skit**

EXPLORE THE BIBLE!

Say: **The bestselling book of all time is right here in my hand.** Hold up a Bible. **Action, adventure, songs, promises, life, love, sacrifice...it's an amazing book! The most amazing thing about the Bible isn't the words that are written in it but who inspired those words to be written. The whole Bible, cover to cover, is true because it comes right from God.** *We trust the Bible because it's from God.* **Listen to this description of the Bible...*from* the Bible!**

Read 2 Timothy 3:14-15. Then shine a flashlight on kids. Say: **Time for an adventure! Spelunkers are people who explore caves.**

Ask: **What are some cool things you might find in a cave?**

We're going spelunking, but not just for [say some of the answers kids just gave]. **Today we're spelunking for truth. I'll need your help!**

Assign roles and have kids act out the skit "The Bible Is the Best!" found at the end of this lesson.

Afterward, lead this discussion:

• **How is learning about the Bible a little like searching for something?**

• **What surprised you about the Scriptures we just heard?**

• **Why do you think God gave us the Bible?**

Talk about: *We trust the Bible because it's from God,* **and we believe God made every part of the Bible fit perfectly together. Only God could inspire different writers at different times in different places to write his words. God loves us so much that he was willing to give us a book with clear directions for how to know him better.**

YARN BARN

Give a piece of yarn to each child, distributing colors randomly. Say: **Let's play a game called "Yarn Barn." Pretend we're on a farm, and this room is our "barn." I'm going to call out directions for certain colors of yarn. If you hear your color, do what I say and fill our "barn" with fun!**

Call out a series of silly directions for each color—for example, "Kids with red yarn, quack like ducks!" Use directions that are both outrageous and fun, and include every color. Here are some fun and silly directions you can use for the different colors:

- Flap your arms like a chicken.

- Crow like a rooster.

- Do your best imitation of a farmer.

- Pretend you're in a pie-eating contest.

- Act like you're any animal that's on a farm.

Afterward, lead this discussion:

- **What was fun about this silly game?**

- **What would've happened if we'd all decided it was too silly or embarrassing to have fun today?**

Say: **Some people think it's silly or embarrassing to follow God's instructions in the Bible. God wants us to have humble hearts that follow him no matter what. Let's see what the Bible says about that.**

Read aloud 2 Peter 1:20-21.

Say: **God—who knows best—is the one who gave us the Bible. When people think something in the Bible is too weird to obey, they're missing out.** *We trust the Bible because it's from God.*

WALK THIS WAY

Set up three to five chairs to form a miniature version of an obstacle course. Call up a volunteer. Say: **Let's explore something else about the Bible with this fun game. See if I can guide you through this obstacle course while you're blindfolded.**

Blindfold your volunteer, and then place him or her at one end of the course. Verbally direct that person through the course, noting when he or she "corrects course" and avoids an obstacle because of your directions.

Afterward ask your volunteer to respond to these questions:

• **What made this easier or harder for you?**

• **What would've happened if you hadn't followed my directions?**

Send your volunteer to join the rest of the class, and then have all kids choose a partner to form pairs. Say: **Now you try it! Take turns being blindfolded and giving directions, and try to guide each other all around the room without bumping into other people or objects.**

Pass out blindfolds and give kids a few minutes to try the activity. Then have partners change roles and try it again.

Afterward, ask:

• **What did you learn about following directions as you did this activity?**

• **What made it easier or harder to trust your partner?**

• **What advice would you give to a brand-new kid who had to play this game?**

Say: **Our partners really helped us succeed by telling us when we were going the wrong way and giving advice to help us go the correct way. Likewise, 2 Timothy 3:16 reminds us that in real life, Scripture "corrects us when we are wrong and teaches us to do what is right." When *we trust the Bible because it's from God* and humbly listen to what the Bible says, we can succeed at life too.**

WHERE'S THE BATHROOM?

YOU'LL NEED:

✓ **Bible**

✓ **paper**

✓ **pencils**

Distribute a pencil and half-sheet of paper to each child.

Say: **I must've had too much water before class! Problem is, now I can't remember where the bathroom is. Maybe you can help me?**

Ask kids to each draw you a map to help you find your way to the bathroom. When maps are ready, collect them all, but give them only a cursory glance.

Say: **Well, I've been thinking. I'm a grown-up, and you all are "just kids." Surely a grown-up knows more than kids, so why should I bother to use these maps you've made?** Toss the maps aside, and then pretend to feel a little discomfort. **Now if only I could remember how to get to the bathroom!**

Ask:

- **What do you think about my prideful attitude toward your maps?**

- **How might a humble attitude help me today?**

Say: **When it comes to the Bible, some people act pridefully like I did. They think they know more than the Bible, or they don't like what they read in the Bible, so they ignore God's Word.**

Ask: **What do _you_ think about that?**

Read aloud 2 Timothy 3:14-17.

Ask: **How might a humble attitude help us gain all the things promised in this Bible verse? Let's brainstorm ideas.**

Allow time for brainstorming ideas.

Say: **It's always helpful if we read the Bible with a humble attitude, not a prideful one. We need to remember that _we trust the Bible because it's from God._**

✓ **1 penny per child**

✓ **1 straw per child**

LIVE IT!

Give each child a penny, and have kids spread out around the room. Say: **In this experiment, you'll have to follow my directions carefully. First, set your coin on the floor in front of you. Without using your hands, your clothes, or any metal, wood, or cardboard tools, make your coin move.**

Give kids a minute to attempt to move their coins. Obviously, no one will succeed.

Hand each child a straw, and say: **Maybe this will help. Try it again, only this time, see if you can figure out how to use the straw to make your coin move. But you can't blow on it or push it with the straw.**

Give kids another minute. Some might figure out how to move the coin. If they don't, explain that they can make it move by placing one end of the straw against the coin and sucking up the air from the other end.

Lead this discussion:

• **What do you think about my directions for moving a penny with a straw?**

• **How do my directions compare with the Bible's directions for life?**

Explain: **Sometimes people give bad or wrong directions. That's never the case with God. In the Bible, God has given us his perfect directions for living—and God's directions are never wrong.** *We trust the Bible because it's from God.*

TAKE-HOME PAGE

Give each child a Take-Home page. Encourage kids to select one of the six challenges for the week ahead.

PRACTICE HUMILITY

Keep growing in your faith and character. Choose one of the following challenges to do this week.

CHALLENGE 1

Pretend you're a TV news reporter and ask friends, family members, or people at church which part of the Bible they like best. Write their answers so you can go read their favorite parts later.

CHALLENGE 2

Be an undercover encourager! Pick a Bible verse you like and write it in a note for a friend or family member. Secretly give the note to the person, and remind him or her that the Bible is trustworthy because it comes from God.

CHALLENGE 3

Draw a picture of your favorite true story from Bible, and give it to a friend or family member. Talk about what's happening in the picture you drew, and tell the person that you believe the Bible because God made it for us.

CHALLENGE 4

Help start a Bible Giveaway program at your church. Ask adults in the congregation to donate Bibles to your children's group so you all can always have Bibles to share with kids who don't have one. Pray that whoever gets a Bible will see it as a light to guide his or her life.

CHALLENGE 5

Write out 2 Peter 1:20-21 on a card or sheet of paper, and put it next to your bed. For one whole week, each night before you go to sleep, hold it under a light and read it. Pray afterward, asking God to help you remember to humbly trust his Word no matter what happens tomorrow.

CHALLENGE 6

Every day for a week, pray, "God, show me how to trust the Bible because it's from you." Write down any experiences you have that you think might be God answering your prayer!

FOR TEACHERS

Write each of the following clues on a separate sheet of paper: "Inspired by God," "Men spoke from God," "God's words," "Read about," and "We believe." Turn the clues over and label each paper with a large number, 1 through 5, in the order of the above phrases.

THE SCENE:
✓ **a cave**

THE SIMPLE SETUP:

Turn off a few lights to create a cave-like atmosphere, and spread the papers number-side up on the floor around the room, or hide them behind classroom objects such as tables and chairs. Make sure you have a Bible for every two kids.

THE CAST:
✓ **Spelunker Leader**
✓ **Spelunker Kids**

THE PROPS:
✓ **Bibles**
✓ **flashlight**
✓ **5 papers with the following written on them:**
"Inspired by God"
"Men spoke from God"
"God's words"
"Read about"
"We believe"

THE BIBLE IS THE BEST!

This skit is a "spelunking" adventure. Kids will "discover" the clues during the skit.

The scene opens with the Spelunker Leader at the front of the audience. The leader is holding a flashlight.

SPELUNKER LEADER
Welcome, spelunkers! We're going to travel deep into this cave to search out clues about where the Bible came from. Since it's kind of dark in here and we only have one flashlight, I'm going to need help. Let's get going!

(The Spelunker Leader starts to move through the audience, shining the flashlight around.)

It's so dark down here! I'm looking for Clue #1. Does anyone see it?

(Encourage the child who finds the paper with the number 1 to stand and read the clue out loud.)

SPELUNKER KID 1
Clue #1 says: "Inspired by God." Check out 2 Timothy 3:16.

Have kids find partners and look up and read 2 Timothy 3:16.

SPELUNKER LEADER
All the words in the Bible are inspired by God. That means God is the author of all the ideas for the stories and words in the Bible. That's our first clue. Now on to Clue #2. Who can find it?

(Encourage the child who finds the paper with the number 2 to stand and read the clue out loud.)

SPELUNKER KID 2
Clue #2 says: "Men spoke from God." To learn more about the truth, read 2 Peter 1:20-21.

Have kids find new partners and look up and read 2 Peter 1:20-21.

SPELUNKER LEADER
God didn't use a pen or a computer to write down his ideas. God chose a whole group of people to write the words for him. He chose men like Moses, David, Luke, Matthew, Mark, John, and Paul.

Great job, Spelunkers! Let's find Clue #3.

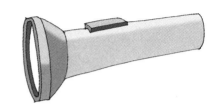

(Encourage the child who finds the paper with the number 3 to stand and read the clue out loud.)

SPELUNKER KID 3
Here's our third clue. It says: "God's words."

SPELUNKER LEADER
God didn't need anyone to approve his ideas. God's ideas were the best ever written.

(Have the children who found them hold up the papers with the clues on them.)

Let's review the clues we've found so far. "Inspired by God," "Men spoke from God," and "God's words." I think we're getting closer to discovering the answer to our question: Where did the Bible come from?

Now I need another spelunker to find Clue #4.

(Encourage the child who finds the paper with the number 4 to stand and read the clue out loud.)

SPELUNKER KID 4
Here's our fourth clue. It says: "Read about."

SPELUNKER LEADER
Since the beginning, God's words in the Bible have been written and read all over the world. Millions and millions of Bibles have been sold in bookstores, read in libraries, and even read online. The Bible is the best book because God wrote it. Now I need one last spelunker kid to find our final clue.

(Encourage the child who finds the paper with the number 5 to stand and read the clue out loud.)

SPELUNKER KID 5

Here's our fifth clue. It says: "We believe." Dig into 2 Timothy 3:17 to learn more.

Have kids find partners and look up and read 2 Timothy 3:17.

SPELUNKER LEADER

The Bible says, "All Scripture is inspired by God and is useful to teach us what is true and to make us realize what is wrong in our lives. It corrects us when we are wrong and teaches us to do what is right. God uses it to prepare and equip his people to do every good work." That means God created the Bible to help us make right choices and love others as he does.

Great job, everyone! Now let's put our clues together to answer our question.

(Encourage all the kids to read the clues in order.)

SPELUNKER KIDS

Inspired by God. Men spoke from God. God's words. Read about. We believe.

SPELUNKER LEADER

That's the answer to our question, "Where did the Bible come from?" God inspired the ideas, men spoke from God using God's words, we read the Bible, and we believe the words are true. Because God wrote all the words in the Bible, we know the Bible is true.

Great job, spelunkers! Thanks for your help. Now we just need to get out of this cave...

WE CAN BE HUMBLE— JUST LIKE JESUS

LEADER PREP

Luke 18:9-14

LESSON AT A GLANCE

There is no better example of true humility than Jesus—and he helped us understand what humility means by sharing the parable of the Pharisee and tax collector. In this story, a Pharisee brags to God about all his accomplishments, while a nearby tax collector kneels before God and humbly prays for mercy. Use this lesson to help your children learn what true humility looks like.

HUMILITY IS...
seeing myself the way God sees me.

WHAT KIDS DO	WHAT YOU'LL NEED
God Sightings *(5 minutes)* Talk about ways they've seen God at work.	
Explore the Bible! *(10 minutes)* Make "I-M-U-R" notes to explore the importance of acting humbly.	• Bible • sticky notes • pencils
Hard Times *(15 minutes)* Watch a video to explore what it means to humbly trust God.	• Bible • *Grow Together Now* DVD • DVD player
Pencil in the Water *(10 minutes)* View an optical effect and compare it to life with a humble attitude.	• 5 long pencils • 1 clear pitcher, half-full of water • flashlight
Is/Is Not *(10 minutes)* Decide which attitudes and actions are humble and which are not.	
Live It! *(15 minutes)* Spend time in a humble posture-prayer session.	

ILLUSTRATED BY PAMELA JOHNSON

Photocopy the Take-Home page at the end of this lesson for each child.

DEVOTIONS FOR LEADERS:

HUMILITY

Invite God to do some spiritual housekeeping in your life. Ask him to root out pride and draw attitudes of arrogance to your attention. Surrender these issues to God, and rely on his mercy and forgiveness. Then look for people you'd normally look down upon, and ask God to show you how you can treat them better, loving them with the humility of Christ.

BIBLE BACKGROUND FOR LEADERS

Luke 18:9-14: The Pharisee and the Tax Collector

OPPOSING CHARACTERS

Jesus sat down with a group of people who "had great confidence in their own righteousness and scorned everyone else." Jesus then crafted a story with a main character who was a lot like his audience: a self-righteous Pharisee. The character Jesus created—a respected religious leader—lived a stunningly upright life; careful to obey God's law, he had complete confidence that God would be pleased with him.

The story's other character, a tax collector, was in an entirely different frame of mind. Jesus doesn't spell out the man's sins, but the audience could have made several assumptions. Tax collectors worked for Rome, collected exorbitant taxes from the Jews, and lined their own pockets by charging extra. Hated by most of the Jewish community, some were even excommunicated from Judaism altogether.

THERE'S NO "I" IN PRAYER

In his prayer, the Pharisee talks mostly about himself—"I" this and "I" that. He even goes so far as to say, "I thank you, God, that I am not a sinner"! We can see the Pharisee's pride in his self-focused prayer and in his disdain for the tax collector praying nearby. On the other hand, modern readers may diagnose the tax collector with a serious case of low self-esteem. He likely had good reason for his self-reproach; he'd probably cheated others and/or lived a greedy life...and he knew it. Unlike the prayer of the overconfident Pharisee, the tax collector's prayer was humble and God-focused.

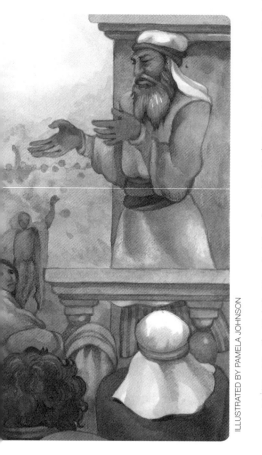

ILLUSTRATED BY PAMELA JOHNSON

This man came to God with a sense of guilt for his sin, relying on the unearned mercy of God.

LESS OF ME, MORE OF YOU

It's easy to misunderstand biblical humility; it's not just feeling bad about oneself or focusing on one's sinfulness. Jesus is the greatest example of humility—and he was sinless. In Scripture we see that Jesus "gave up his divine privileges" (Philippians 2:7) so that he could take on the humble position of a servant. We can follow Jesus' example by doing the same, having less of "us" and more of "him." Jesus' parable isn't meant to make us feel unworthy; instead, it challenges us to have a mindset that's God-focused, not self-focused.

THE LESSON

GOD SIGHTINGS

Use the text below or substitute your own examples for this weekly lesson-starter activity.

Say: **James 1:17 in the Bible reminds us that "Whatever is good and perfect is a gift coming down to us from God our Father." That means the gift of a beautiful sunset is evidence of God at. When your friend shares with you, that's God's kindness at work. When you smile at others or hold open a door, you're showing God's joy.**

It's important that we recognize and thank God for the ways we see him all around us and the ways he is at work in our lives. We call these God Sightings.

Ask: **How have you seen God at work this week? What evidence have you seen of God's creativity, joy, forgiveness, and goodness?**

Think about God's creation, ways people have encouraged you, and even ways God helped you make a difference for someone else.

As a group, share God Sightings. Then celebrate God's gifts in your lives with a prayer of thanksgiving.

YOU'LL NEED:

✓ **Bible**
✓ **sticky notes**
✓ **pencils**

EXPLORE THE BIBLE!

Open this activity by saying: **When we pray, God knows what we need and knows what's in our hearts. That means we can act humbly when we approach God, which helps us humbly encourage others after we're done praying. Let's read about two men's prayers in the Bible and see if we can discover more about that.**

Read aloud Luke 18:10-12.

Ask: **What stands out most to you about this man's prayer?**

Read aloud Luke 18:13-14.

Ask: **What stands out most to you about *this* man's prayer?**

Say: **The tax collector was humble while praying. The Pharisee was not.**

Ask: **Why do you think that would be important to Jesus?**

Say: **Jesus was always humble, and *we can be humble—just like Jesus.* Let's try a little activity to help us practice that.**

Give each child two sticky notes and a pencil. Explain: **We're going to do a project called "I–M–U–R." Here's how it goes. First, we know God gives everyone gifts and talents. Maybe you're really good at math, you can run really fast, or you're really funny. Write the letters "I" and "M" at the top of a sticky note, and then on that note write one gift or talent you have. If it's easier for you to draw a picture, that's okay.**

Have kids stick their notes on themselves somewhere. Then have each child find a partner to form pairs. Have partners take a moment to share their notes with each other.

Next say: **On another sticky note, write the letters "U" and "R" and then something you admire about your partner.**

Have kids each stick their "U-R" notes on top of their partner's "I-M" stickies. Check to be sure every child gets a "U-R" note.

Afterward, lead this discussion:

- **Think about the Pharisee and the tax collector from Luke 18. How do you think they would've handled this activity? Describe your thoughts to your partner.**

- **In what ways did this activity show you that you can act humbly, like the tax collector did?**

- **How did it make you feel to humbly encourage someone else with a "U-R" note? Explain.**

Say: **When we have a humble attitude before God, like the tax collector, that makes it easier for us to act humbly toward our friends and family. Plus, it gives us the power to encourage others.**

HARD TIMES

Say: **There's another passage in the Bible that tells about a man who was humble before Jesus.**

Read aloud Matthew 8:5-10,13.

Share with kids: **Nobody loves you as much as Jesus does. When we're humble and ask for his help, he'll always be there for us. Let me show you an example of what I mean.**

Show "Hard Times" (track 1) from the *Grow Together Now* DVD.

Afterward, lead this discussion:

- **What did you notice about the Roman officer in this video?**

- **How do you think this might have ended if the Roman officer had marched up to Jesus and demanded healing for his servant?**

- **What does this story teach you and me about facing hard times? Let's brainstorm at least five things.**

Wrap up by saying: **Jesus is always humble and helpful, and he wants each of us to humbly trust him, even when it's hard. When we're facing a tough time, *we can be humble— just like Jesus.* That's what the Roman officer did, and it changed everything for him!**

YOU'LL NEED:

✓ **Bible**
✓ ***Grow Together Now* DVD**
✓ **DVD player**

✓ **5 long pencils**

✓ **1 clear pitcher, half-full of water**

✓ **flashlight**

PENCIL IN THE WATER

Say: **When we humbly trust the Bible because it's from God, we can see things from God's point of view. Then God helps us see life in a new light and understand better what is possible. Let's try an experiment about light and see if that can help us understand this better.**

Show everyone the five pencils you brought. Point out how straight and firm they look. Next, set a clear pitcher, half-full of water, on a table where everyone can see it. (If your class has fewer than six kids, just invite everyone to gather around the pitcher for a closer look.) Then darken your room as much as possible.

Say: **Light travels in straight lines, which are called light rays. If you point a flashlight ahead of you, the light will always be in front of you. You can count on it. But that's not all there is to light.**

Partially submerge the pencils in the water. Shine your flashlight on the water. The result will be a visual phenomenon that causes the pencils to appear warped in the water.

Ask:

• **What do you see? Describe it.**

• **Shining light on the water changed the way the pencils looked. Why do you think that's important for us to notice?**

Say: **Jesus was always humble, and when we are humble like he was, it's like letting his light shine through our lives.**

Ask this question to wrap up the experiment: **What do you think might change if we tried to live with a humble attitude like Jesus, letting his light shine in and through us every day?**

IS/IS NOT

Say: *We can be humble like Jesus*, but sometimes it's hard to know what that looks like. Let's see if we can help each other figure it out.

Point to opposite walls in your room. Designate one wall as "Is," and the other as "Is Not." Read aloud the situations below (and add a few specific to your church too), and ask kids to stand by one of the walls to rate whether they believe that act is humble or not. Encourage kids to voice opinions about why they chose as they did and to give advice for people in the situations.

Is or is not?

- Both Erik and Jody want to watch TV. Erik says he's the *Not* oldest, so he gets to pick the show.

- Before going to sleep at night, Asia thinks about people *IS* she loves and asks God to help them.

- Chad-Michael seems to be the best at everything, so he *Not* tries to be first all the time.

- Dana is pretty good at math, so she sometimes tutors *IS* her friends who aren't as good at it as she is.

- Leila likes to stand at the door and greet people when *IS* they come to church.

- Greer always keeps his headphones on when talking to *NOT* his parents.

- Most nights, Davis chooses to play video games instead of eating dinner with his mom.

- Allie likes it when her baby brother laughs, so she tries to spend time playing with him every day.

- Randi prays to be more like Jesus every day.

Say: *We can be humble—just like Jesus.* Sometimes that's as simple as paying attention to our attitudes, and asking ourselves, **"Is this humble or not?"**

LIVE IT!

Say: **Spending time in prayer every day is one great way that *we can be humble—just like Jesus.*** **There are lots of different ways to pray. Some prayers are for other people, some are for you, some are to say thanks, and sometimes we pray just to feel nearer to God. So let's spend time in humble prayer right now.**

Lead kids in a posture-prayer as follows.

Have kids stand and raise their arms. Say: **Take a moment to tell God thanks for the way he loves you. Thank him for a few specific things you like in your life.**

Have each child lower his or her arms and wrap them around his or her upper body. Say: **Tell Jesus what you're worried about right now. Ask him for help.**

Have kids kneel in place and lay their arms, palms face up, at their sides. Say: **Mention to God a family member or friend you care about. Ask God to help that person and to show you how you can help too.**

While kneeling, have kids lean their heads forward toward the floor and place their palms on the ground. Say: **Ask Jesus to help you understand how near he is to you right now and always.**

After prayer, lead this discussion to end your time together:

- **Say one word that describes how you feel after our prayer time just now.**

- **Why do you think it was important for us to act humbly toward God during our prayer?**

- **What can we do this week to help us remember to spend more time in humble prayer? Let's brainstorm ideas.** Be sure to share your own ideas as kids brainstorm.

TAKE-HOME PAGE

Give each child a Take-Home page. Encourage kids to select one of the six challenges for the week ahead.

PRACTICE HUMILITY

Keep growing in your faith and character. Choose one of the following challenges to do this week.

CHALLENGE 1

It's humbling when you look for ways to make others feel better. Today, find a friend and share something awesome that you see about him or her.

CHALLENGE 2

Be sneaky about your humility! In other words, find ways to help others feel better without getting praise in return. Clean the kitchen while your family is in the other room, or leave the first controller for others when playing a video game. See if you can go the whole day without bragging about things.

CHALLENGE 3

At the end of the day, tell God where you messed up. It's a humbling experience, talking about your faults. Be humble and truthful before God, and ask for forgiveness, if necessary. The good news: He loves you no matter what.

CHALLENGE 4

Read about Daniel in Daniel 6:10 and Daniel 10:12, and list all the ways you see that he acted humbly toward God and others.

CHALLENGE 5

Try a trick called "thank you praise." When someone gives you a compliment, thank him or her for the compliment and then thank God for the gifts he's given you. For example, if someone pays you the compliment of "Wow! You're a really great musician!" reply with "Thank you." Then thank God for giving you the gift of a musical ability.

CHALLENGE 6

Every day for a week, pray, "God, show me how to be humble—just like Jesus." Write down any experiences you have that you think might be God answering your prayer!

LESSON 2 | WE CAN BE HUMBLE—JUST LIKE JESUS

HUMBLE HEROES RELY ON GOD FOR STRENGTH

LEADER PREP

1 Samuel 17:1-50

LESSON AT A GLANCE

Sometimes we face problems that seem really big. David had a big problem—and its name was Goliath. Just like David, your kids have had to struggle against "Goliaths." David trusted God to help him. Use this lesson to teach children that just as God helped David be strong, God can give them strength, too.

HUMILITY IS...
seeing myself the way God sees me.

WHAT KIDS DO	WHAT YOU'LL NEED
God Sightings *(5 minutes)* Talk about ways they've seen God at work.	
Explore the Bible! *(10 minutes)* Mirror-read the Bible account to better understand and relate to what happened.	• Bible
Facing Our Goliaths *(15 minutes)* Watch a video about kids dealing with big problems, and explore how they face problems too.	• *Grow Together Now* DVD • DVD player
Tornado in a Bottle *(10 minutes)* Create a miniature tornado as a prompt for prayer.	• small, empty water bottles—enough for each child to have 1 • pitcher of water • liquid dishwashing soap
Balloon Bop *(10 minutes)* Play a balloon game that reveals a helpful principle of Christian living.	• 5 colorful balloons, inflated • marker
Live It! *(15 minutes)* Create a reminder to rely on Jesus in hard times.	• blank labels, about the size of a name tag *(available at your local office supply store)* • markers or crayons

ILLUSTRATED BY DREW KREVI

Photocopy the Take-Home page at the end of this lesson for each child.

29

DEVOTIONS FOR LEADERS:

HUMILITY

The account of David and Goliath is a favorite among children who like to see the "little guy" come out on top. How can we not be inspired when God works a miracle through a mere boy? Armed with faith, David faced a challenge of gigantic proportions—and won. Similarly, no matter what issues we face, Jesus is our strength and shield. A relationship with Jesus can give us confidence. Living out our faith is our testimony to a Lord who is mightier than any Goliath. What calling do you have that others may think you're "too small" for? Pray that Jesus will give you the courage to overcome doubters, and pray that you'll be able to communicate his faithfulness as you teach this lesson.

BIBLE BACKGROUND FOR LEADERS

1 Samuel 17:1-50: David Defeats Goliath

STRATEGIC POSITIONING

When the Philistine and Israelite armies gathered their troops for battle at the valley of Elah, they settled on opposite hills and lingered, watching each other for 40 days without attacking. This may seem like an odd tactic, but if either army rushed down its hill and across the valley to attack first, that army would likely suffer tremendous casualties. So each army waited for the other.

A SCARY ADVERSARY

In ancient times, when "war champions" such as Goliath were designated to fight as representatives of their armies, the outcome of the entire battle was to rest on that one fight. However, armies believed that the results of the fight were controlled more by the warriors' gods than by the strength or cunning of the warriors themselves. Saul apparently wasn't confident enough in God to face Goliath. Fortunately, David was!

DAVID FIGHTS THE ODDS

David's willingness to fight Goliath is remarkable on several counts: First, he was a shepherd boy of about 16 years, not an experienced warrior. In addition, he entered the fight under the mocking ridicule of his older brother who, though afraid to face Goliath himself, accused David of chasing fame and glory. Finally,

ILLUSTRATED BY RONNIE ROONEY

while the giant was outfitted with armor, sword, spear, and javelin, David rejected the offer of King Saul's own armor and weaponry, preferring nothing but the armor of faith.

DAVID RELIES ON GOD FOR VICTORY

Imagine the Israelites' tension as they watched an inexperienced boy determine the outcome of their entire battle. And imagine the adrenaline coursing through this young shepherd as he charged the lumbering giant, wielding only a slingshot and a mighty faith in God! We know how it ends. Shouting a tribute to the Lord of heaven's armies, David defeated the giant with a single shot from his sling, securing victory for the entire army of Israel. God honored David's faith with triumph.

THE LESSON

GOD SIGHTINGS

Use the text below or substitute your own examples for this weekly lesson-starter activity.

Say: **James 1:17 in the Bible reminds us that "Whatever is good and perfect is a gift coming down to us from God our Father." That means the gift of a beautiful sunset is evidence of God. When your friend shares with you, that's God's kindness at work. When you smile at others or hold open a door, you're showing God's joy.**

It's important that we recognize and thank God for the ways we see him all around us and the ways he is at work in our lives. We call these God Sightings.

Ask: **How have you seen God at work this week? What evidence have you seen of God's creativity, joy, forgiveness, and goodness?**

Think about God's creation, ways people have encouraged you, and even ways God helped you make a difference for someone else.

As a group, share God Sightings. Then celebrate God's gifts in your lives with a prayer of thanksgiving.

EXPLORE THE BIBLE!

Say: **We're going to dig into the Bible right now, but this time instead of just reading it, we're going "mirror-read" it. That'll help us better understand, and relate to, what really happened. Here's how this works.**

Call two volunteer actors to the front. (Try to pick volunteers who are outgoing and not afraid of performing in front of a group.) Assign one actor the role of David and the other the role of Goliath. Tell "David" and "Goliath" that their jobs are to act out what happens as you read the Scripture.

Next, tell kids on the left side of your classroom that they are David-Mirrors, and their job is to copy whatever they see the "David" actor doing. Likewise, kids on the right side of the room are Goliath-Mirrors who should copy whatever they see the "Goliath" actor doing.

When everyone is ready, read aloud 1 Samuel 17:1-50. It's a long passage, so be sure to break up the story by pausing in strategic spots and letting your actors perform.

Afterward, lead this discussion:

- **What was it like for you to be David? or for you to be Goliath? Explain.**

- **What did you learn about David or Goliath from mirroring their actions in the Bible?**

- **Why wasn't Goliath more humble when David came out to face him?**

- **How did David show himself to be a humble hero of God? Give examples.**

Wrap up this teaching segment by saying: **David gives us a great example of the truth that *humble heroes rely on God for strength.***

FACING OUR GOLIATHS

Say: **David was a young Bible hero challenged with a giant-sized problem. Let's see what other young people have to say about challenges they face in their lives.**

Show "Facing our Goliaths" (track 2) from the *Grow Together Now* DVD.

Afterward, lead this discussion:

- **What are you thinking about after watching these stories?**

- **Talk about a time you felt scared or faced something that was hard. What happened?** Share an example from your own life; then let kids share.

- *Humble heroes rely on God for strength.* **How do they do that?**

Say: **Sometimes giant-sized problems seem impossible to beat. We might feel the way the kids did in the video. But like those kids, we can remember that *humble heroes rely on God for strength*. When God is on our side, those problems might not seem quite so big after all!**

TORNADO IN A BOTTLE

Say: **Let's do something different now—let's see if we can create a tornado in a bottle!**

Give every child an empty water bottle. Then use your pitcher of water to fill each bottle partway. Finally, add a single drop of liquid dishwashing soap to each water bottle. Warn kids not to drink it! Make sure each child securely fastens the lid on his or her water bottle.

Say: **Think of what you know about tornados: They can be very powerful; they can pick up cars and damage buildings; if a tornado hits, we take shelter because it can really mess things up in a community.**

Tell kids that by holding the cap and spinning their bottles in a circular motion, they can create "mini-tornadoes" in the bottles. Have kids try it.

Ask: **When was a time you felt upset or scared or worried— so much so that it felt like a tornado was blowing through your life? What happened?**

Say: **When situations come that shake up our lives, Jesus wants us to be humble heroes who pray for help.**

✓ **small, empty water bottles—enough for each child to have 1**

✓ **pitcher of water**

✓ **liquid dishwashing soap**

Have kids gently shake up their bottles again, and ask: **What might you want to say to Jesus next time it feels like a mini-tornado is happening to you?**

Say: **Let's pray some of those things now.** Lead children in praying about situations they mentioned, and use their ideas in answer to the previous question as part of your prayer.

Finish this moment by saying: *Humble heroes rely on God for strength.* **When you need strength in the future, remember your mini-tornado and take time to humbly ask Jesus for help.**

BALLOON BOP

Say: **When David went out to face Goliath, he took along five smooth stones for battle. Well, we can't throw stones in here, so I've brought five smooth balloons instead. We're going to use them to play a game called "Balloon Bop," but first let's brainstorm a bit.**

Ask kids to brainstorm at least five ways God gives us strength—for instance, through Bible promises, help from his Holy Spirit, prayer, and Christian friends. Write the five best brainstorm ideas on the balloons, one idea.per balloon. Then invite kids to form a circle and play "Balloon Bop."

Explain: **The rules for "Balloon Bop" are easy. I'll stand in the middle of the circle and toss the balloons in the air. You just have to do your best to keep the balloons from touching the floor. Ready, set...wait a minute!**

Tell kids you need to add one tiny little rule: While you stand in the middle, they all have to face away from you, and kids must keep their eyes shut at all times during the game. When they're in position, shout "Go!" and toss the balloons in the air. Obviously, the balloons will fall to the ground pretty quickly.

Express disappointment at how poorly the kids played the first round of this game. Then play a second round, this time allowing kids to face you and to keep their eyes open. They should perform much better! Play as many rounds as time allows; then gather kids for discussion.

Ask:

- **What did you think about trying to play this game with your eyes closed?**

- Why was it easier to play this game when you were able to keep your eyes on the balloons?

- What can we learn from this game to help us when we need strength from God in our daily lives?

Say: *Humble heroes rely on God for strength.* **That's a lot easier to do when we keep our eyes on him and pay attention to the ways God has provided to give us strength.**

LIVE IT!

Say: *Humble heroes rely on God for strength,* **but I'm going to be honest and tell you that sometimes that will be hard for you. Sometimes you'll try to handle a problem all by yourself, or you'll feel like the problem is so big that you just want to give up.**

Ask: **Name some situations when you might feel like that— or maybe even a time you *have* felt like that?**

Allow a few kids to respond. Then pass out the blank labels, one for each child, along with a marker or crayon for each child.

Say: **When you feel like it's hard to rely on God for strength, remember this saying: "I can't do it...Jesus can!" Let me show you a simple way to help you remember that.**

Lead kids in the following: **Draw the letter "I" on your blank label. Look at that letter and say out loud, "I can't do it..."** (Pause for kids to say it.) **Then cross out the "I" by putting a line right through the middle of it. Do you see what you've made? It's a cross, a reminder of Jesus! Now you can say out loud, "Jesus can!"** (Pause for kids to shout.)

Say: **Make this little drawing anytime you feel overwhelmed or anytime you just need strength from God.**

Have kids place their new labels on each other and then close your class session in prayer.

TAKE-HOME PAGE

Give each child a Take-Home page. Encourage kids to select one of the six challenges for the week ahead.

YOU'LL NEED:

✓ **blank labels, about the size of a name tag** *(available at your local office supply store)*

✓ **markers or crayons**

PRACTICE HUMILITY

Keep growing in your faith and character. Choose one of the following challenges to do this week.

CHALLENGE 1

Ask a parent or grandparent about a time God gave him or her strength in the past.

CHALLENGE 2

Do you know someone who doesn't believe in God? Rely on God's strength to help you tell him or her about God and why you rely on God.

CHALLENGE 3

Once a day, look in a mirror and flex your muscles. Pray, "God, help me be a humble hero and rely on you for strength!"

CHALLENGE 4

Look up 1 Samuel 17:1-50 in your Bible. Imagine you are a newspaper cartoonist, and a national newspaper wants you to make a daily comic strip out of this story. What would it look like? How many days would it run? Go ahead and try it!

CHALLENGE 5

Teach someone you love how to use the "I can't do it…Jesus can!" reminder drawing you learned in class this week. Use it to help you both practice relying on God at all times.

CHALLENGE 6

Every day for a week, pray, "God, show me how to be a humble hero who relies on you." Write down any experiences you have that you think might be God answering your prayer!

WE'RE CONTENT WITH WHAT GOD GIVES US

LEADER PREP

2 Samuel 12:1-6

LESSON AT A GLANCE

Nathan the prophet told King David a story about a rich man who stole a young lamb from a poor man. While the rich man had many livestock, the lamb had been the poor man's only possession. Through this story, God showed David that he should be content with what God has given him and not seek other people's things. Use this lesson to help your children learn to humbly accept God's provision.

HUMILITY IS...
seeing myself the way God sees me.

WHAT KIDS DO	WHAT YOU'LL NEED
God Sightings *(5 minutes)* Talk about ways they've seen God at work.	
Explore the Bible! *(10 minutes)* See what happens when cotton-ball sheep are unfairly taken away.	• 1 cotton ball per child
Complain Game *(15 minutes)* Invent creative complaints, and compare that to finding satisfaction in life.	• 3 chairs
Written on the Walls *(10 minutes)* Create a thankfulness mural as a reminder to be content.	• large sheet(s) of craft paper *(white or brown)* or poster board • tape • colorful markers • colorful stickers
Rich Man, Poor Man *(10 minutes)* Watch a video that retells the Bible story, and explore what it means together.	• *Grow Together Now* DVD • DVD player
Live It! *(15 minutes)* Encourage each other with ideas for how to live with contentment during the week.	• 3x5 cards • pencils

Photocopy the Take-Home page at the end of this lesson for each child.

ILLUSTRATED BY RONNIE ROONEY

DON'T TAKE WHAT ISN'T YOURS

DEVOTIONS FOR LEADERS:

HUMILITY

Overcoming the desire for more and learning contentment are struggles even for a man after God's own heart (1 Samuel 13:14). What trips you up in the "more" department? Money, clothes, gadgets, even food? The world works to convince us we need more than we have and that we won't be happy until we have it. In the face of temptation to gain by your own means, make this your prayer of contentment to our generous God: "Give me neither poverty nor riches! Give me just enough to satisfy my needs" (Proverbs 30:8).

BIBLE BACKGROUND FOR LEADERS

2 Samuel 12:1-6: Nathan Gives David a Message From God

INSPIRED BY TRUE EVENTS

King David quickly spiraled downward into a pit of sin. What started with a clandestine glance snowballed into adultery, lies, and eventually murder (2 Samuel 11). Only a handful of people would've known what David had done—and none would've confronted him. With Uriah dead and Bathsheba's period of mourning over (2 Samuel 11:27), David attempted to make things right by bringing her to the palace to give birth to their son. It should've been a joyous occasion, but David's actions were about to catch up with him. The Lord was displeased with what David had done. So the Lord sent Nathan the prophet to tell David this story (2 Samuel 11:27–12:1).

THE MAN IN THE MIRROR

Nathan spun a yarn about two men, one rich, one poor, and their possessions—or lack thereof. "The rich man owned a great many sheep and cattle. The poor man owned nothing but one little lamb he had bought." David didn't ask why Nathan came to visit or why he told this story. We can assume David listened intently, gauging by his outrage when he heard Nathan's end to the tale: The rich man stole and killed the poor man's only lamb to serve to a dinner guest. To David, the injustice was obvious, and just punishment demanded severity. He even wished he could sentence the rich man to death rather than settling for the restitution outlined in the Law. What David didn't see was his own reflection in the story.

Nathan wiped away the grime from the metaphorical mirror and made his message clear: "You are that man!"

THE MORAL OF THE STORY

Television ads for knives and cookware entice viewers by sweetening the deal: "But wait...there's more!" Through Nathan, God reminded David of all he'd been given—palaces, wives, kingdoms. But wait...there's more! God didn't stop there. "And if that had not been enough, I would have given you much, much more" (2 Samuel 12:8). If David wasn't content with what he had, he would've only had to ask. Jesus described God's giving nature as that of a parent who gives his children the best. "If you sinful people know how to give good gifts to your children, how much more will your heavenly Father give good gifts to those who ask him" (Matthew 7:11). David gave in to desiring more and went about getting it the wrong way—but the good news is he repented and God forgave him (2 Samuel 12:13). David paid a high price for his sins, but he was a changed man who later gave generously out of his private treasures for the building of the Temple.

THE LESSON

GOD SIGHTINGS

Use the text below or substitute your own examples for this weekly lesson-starter activity.

Say: **James 1:17 in the Bible reminds us that "Whatever is good and perfect is a gift coming down to us from God our Father." That means the gift of a beautiful sunset is evidence of God. When your friend shares with you, that's God's kindness at work. When you smile at others or hold open a door, you're showing God's joy.**

It's important that we recognize and thank God for the ways we see him all around us and the ways he is at work in our lives. We call these God Sightings.

Ask: **How have you seen God at work this week? What evidence have you seen of God's creativity, joy, forgiveness, and goodness?**

Think about God's creation, ways people have encouraged you, and even ways God helped you make a difference for someone else.

As a group, share God Sightings. Then celebrate God's gifts in your lives with a prayer of thanksgiving.

EXPLORE THE BIBLE!

Give each child a cotton ball.

Tell everyone that their cotton balls are all "pet sheep." Encourage kids to name their sheep, to teach them tricks (like "sheep, jump over my finger"), and to show them off to each other. Give children a moment for this; then call everyone back together.

Have kids stand. Say: **All right. Here's a new rule: Anyone wearing red can take a sheep from any other person in the room. If someone takes your cotton ball, sit down.**

See how many children are left standing. Then say: **Now, this is for anyone who is still standing. If your birthday is in December, January, or February, you can take sheep from anyone whose birthday is not in those months. If someone takes your cotton ball, sit down.**

See how many kids are left standing, and then ask which of them is the youngest. Say: **The youngest person standing can take everyone else's sheep. If your cotton ball is taken, sit down.**

Have the last person standing come up to stand by you. Ask the group to respond to these questions:

- **How do you feel about this person who took all your sheep right now? Explain.**

- **Why did you care whether or not your cotton ball was taken?**

Send your cotton-ball king back to his or her seat. Say: **It kind of stunk to have someone take away your cotton ball unfairly. Believe it or not, something similar once happened with King David in the Bible. Before this event happened, there's something you need to know about King David. He had decided he wanted another man's wife to be *his* wife. So he sent the other guy to the most dangerous part of a battle, and the man died. Then David married that man's wife. A few months later, this is what happened.**

Read aloud 2 Samuel 12:1-6.

Ask:

- **What are you thinking after hearing what happened with David?**

- **David was the richest, most powerful man in Israel. Why do you think he wasn't content with what he already had?**

- **What advice would you give to David if he were here right now?**

Say: **King David and our cotton-ball sheep can both teach us something very important about life: It's always best when *we're content with what God gives us.***

COMPLAIN GAME

Form three teams of children. (A team can be one person, if needed.) Place three "contestant chairs" up front. Call up a volunteer from each team to be the first contestants.

Explain: **We're going to play the "Complain Game"! One contestant from each team will play each round, earning points for his or her team. I'm going to read a situation; then each contestant must come up with the most creative complaint about that situation. For instance, if I said, "You're going to Disneyland!" your complaint might be "That's no fun—I'll probably fall off a roller coaster and land on Mickey Mouse!" I'll give 100 points to the contestant with the most creative complaint each round. Ready? Let's get started!**

Play several rounds of the Complain Game, giving every child a chance to be a contestant.

Ask:

- **What would it be like to be around someone who *really* complained like that? Explain.**

- **What's it like to be around someone who's content instead of complaining?**

Say: **That was fun as a game, but it'd be really tiring in real life. Sadly, some people seem to think they'll get a prize** for complaining! We don't have to be like that when *we're content with what God gives us.*

WRITTEN ON THE WALLS

Say: **One way to remember to be content is to think about everything you have to be thankful for. Let's create something to help us do that.**

Lay out a large sheet of craft paper (white or brown) or poster board where all kids can access it. Pass out colorful markers and stickers. Encourage kids to use the supplies to create a group mural suitable for display in your classroom. Tell kids the theme is "Contentment" and to draw whatever would represent things for which they are thankful.

For example, kids might draw their families, homes, schools, friends, pets, sports, or comic books.

When they're done, say: **Look at all the things God has done for us! This is a great reminder that it's always best when *we're content with what God gives us.***

Tape the mural to a wall, and leave it up for the next two weeks as a classroom reminder.

RICH MAN, POOR MAN

Tell kids: **As we've discovered, King David was a great man and a great ruler, but he made a really bad choice. David liked another man's wife—he liked her so much that he wanted her to be his wife. So he did an unbelievable thing: He had the man killed! Because of this awful choice, God knew David needed to be shown that he'd done wrong, so God sent the prophet Nathan to tell David a story about a rich man, a poor man, and a little lamb. Let's watch a video that retells that story in a creative way.**

Show "Rich Man, Poor Man" (track 3) from the *Grow Together Now* DVD.

Afterward, lead this discussion:

- **Tell about a time someone took something from you—or you wanted to take something that belonged to someone**

YOU'LL NEED:

- ✓ **large sheet(s) of craft paper (white or brown) or poster board**
- ✓ **tape**
- ✓ **colorful markers**
- ✓ **colorful stickers**

YOU'LL NEED:

- ✓ ***Grow Together Now* DVD**
- ✓ **DVD player**

---

else. What happened? Share an example from your own life; then let kids tell their stories.

- **Why do people take things from others?**

- **When is it hard for you to be happy with what you have?**

Say: **In Nathan's story, even though the rich man had many sheep, he took the poor man's lamb. The rich man had more than enough. He didn't need to take something that didn't belong to him. God gives us what we need, and we can be thankful for what we have.** *We're content with what God gives us,* **and that means our stuff can always be good enough.**

LIVE IT!

YOU'LL NEED:

✓ **3x5 cards**
✓ **pencils**

Say: **Let's finish out today's lesson with something I call "The Idea Shuffle."**

Have kids form pairs, and give every pair two 3x5 cards and pencils. (You may want to pair younger kids with older ones who can help them for this activity.) Instruct kids to work together in their pairs to brainstorm ideas that could help a friend remember to be content this week. Ideas might include Scripture quotes, prayer prompts, or encouraging notes.

Tell kids to write their two best ideas on the 3x5 cards—one idea per card. (Older kids can help younger kids who need help with writing.)

When everyone is ready, collect all the cards. Say: **Now it's time for the "shuffle"!** Mix up all the cards, and then redistribute them randomly—one to each person (it's okay if a child gets his or her own card back).

Say: **Take your idea home and tape it to your bathroom mirror for one week. Let it remind you that** *we're content with what God gives us.*

Close your class session with prayer.

TAKE-HOME PAGE

Give each child a Take-Home page. Encourage kids to select one of the six challenges for the week ahead.

PRACTICE HUMILITY

Keep growing in your faith and character. Choose one of the following challenges to do this week.

CHALLENGE 1

Ask your parents to help you look up how to say thank you in different languages on the internet. Write "thank you" in English and a few other languages, and tape the list to your wall so it can remind you to be thankful for what God has given you.

CHALLENGE 2

Ask your parents to help you find pictures of underdeveloped countries. Then compare those to pictures of rich or wealthy societies. Discuss how there will always be people who are less or more fortunate than you. Give thanks for what God has given you.

CHALLENGE 3

Look around your house and say "thank you" to God for everything you have: your bed, sheets, pillow, food, dinner table, and toys. Consider how each thing helps you—and what life would be like without those things.

CHALLENGE 4

Make a "Little Lamb" snack for a sibling or friend. Use popcorn for the feet and head, marshmallows for the body, and toothpicks for the legs and neck. Tell what you learned from the story of the rich man taking the poor man's sheep. Explain that God wants us to be thankful for what we have instead of focusing on what we don't.

CHALLENGE 5

Look up and read Philippians 4:11-13 in the Bible. Then take time to write in a journal what it would look like for you to be completely content with what God's given you.

CHALLENGE 6

Every day for a week, pray, "God, teach me how to be more content with what you give me." Write down any experiences you have that you think might be God answering your prayer!

WE LOVE OTHERS BECAUSE GOD LOVES US

LEADER PREP

1 John 4:7-21

LESSON AT A GLANCE

God loves us so much that he sent Jesus to die to take away our sins. Since he loves us that much, we can show others God's love. Sometimes we don't feel like loving some people, but we need to remember God's love for us to help us love them. Use this lesson to help your children learn to love others because God loves us!

KINDNESS IS...
treating others as beloved creations of God.

WHAT KIDS DO	WHAT YOU'LL NEED
God Sightings (5 minutes) Talk about ways they've seen God at work.	
Explore the Bible! (10 minutes) Clap when they hear the word "love" in Scripture, and discuss what that means.	• Bibles • whiteboard or sheet of poster board • marker
Sev's Story (15 minutes) Watch a video about people experiencing God's love, and explore how to show God's love to others.	• *Grow Together Now* DVD • DVD player
How Do You Know? (10 minutes) Identify why they know God loves them and why others know they are loved.	• paper • pencils
Would You Rather...? (10 minutes) Play a game of choices, and talk about how to choose to love.	• masking tape • colorful duct tape
Live It! (15 minutes) Create love notes to share with friends.	• Bible • paper • envelopes • crayons or markers

ILLUSTRATED BY RONNIE ROONEY

Photocopy the Take-Home page at the end of this lesson for each child.

DEVOTIONS FOR LEADERS:

KINDNESS

God is love. That knowledge is ingrained in most of us. In fact, we've heard it so often that perhaps we take the weight of those three little words for granted. God proved his love by sending Jesus to live among us and in us, and he asks that we not only love Jesus but that we spread that love throughout the world. Sharing Jesus' love with others is one way to live our faith inside out.

Are there opportunities for you to minister to others in your life? Ask for God's guidance as you help your children discover his love and learn how to share it with others.

BIBLE BACKGROUND FOR LEADERS

1 John 4:7-21: John Teaches About God's Love

GOD'S LOVE THROUGH JESUS

Our passage in 1 John is full of truths we can live by and use to test the beliefs we face around us. The first truth to emphasize is that of the centrality of Jesus. Simply put, Jesus came to die on the cross so that humans could have a relationship with God. John uses the word *Savior* only twice in all his biblical writings, and both times it is connected with "of the world." John wants to be clear that salvation isn't just for a limited few but for all who believe in Jesus.

LIVING OUT GOD'S LOVE

The second truth we find in 1 John is that of love. When John suggests that living in love is proof that God is living in us, he's not talking about a warm, fuzzy feeling of affection. It's love that focuses obedient attention on God, love that accepts love from God above, and love that works itself out in love toward others. The source of all that love is God, but the proof that he is living in us is that his love pours out from us in all our relationships. And the continued growth in love as described in 1 John 4:17-18 proves that God is living in the Christian, making him or her more and more like Christ, the perfect example of love.

DISCERNING THE TRUE SOURCE

The negative side of this proof is described in 1 John 4:20. If someone doesn't show love to others, particularly Christian

ILLUSTRATED BY PAMELA JOHNSON

brothers or sisters, then that person's relationship with God is suspect. He or she may not really be in a committed relationship with God through Christ. These proofs give us a great start in testing other beliefs. For example, if other beliefs don't pass the "Jesus test" and the "love test," there can't be much truth in them.

THE LESSON

GOD SIGHTINGS

Use the text below or substitute your own examples for this weekly lesson-starter activity.

Say: **James 1:17 in the Bible reminds us that "Whatever is good and perfect is a gift coming down to us from God our Father." That means the gift of a beautiful sunset is evidence of God. When your friend shares with you, that's God's kindness at work. When you smile at others or hold open a door, you're showing God's joy.**

It's important that we recognize and thank God for the ways we see him all around us and the ways he is at work in our lives. We call these God Sightings.

Ask: **How have you seen God at work this week? What evidence have you seen of God's creativity, joy, forgiveness, and goodness?**

Think about God's creation, ways people have encouraged you, and even ways God helped you make a difference for someone else.

As a group, share God Sightings. Then celebrate God's gifts in your lives with a prayer of thanksgiving.

EXPLORE THE BIBLE!

Say: *We love others because God loves us!* **But you don't have to just take my word for it—let's hear what the Bible says about that. I'm going to read 1 John 4:7-21. While I'm reading, why don't you "count the love"?**

Instruct kids to applaud every time they hear you say the word "love" as you read, and ask a volunteer to mark it down on the

YOU'LL NEED:

✓ **Bibles**

✓ **whiteboard or sheet of poster board**

✓ **marker**

whiteboard (or poster board) every time as well. Then read aloud 1 John 4:7-21, pausing for applause as needed. When you're done, invite everyone to give a standing ovation, just for fun.

Say: **Look at how many times "love" was mentioned in this Bible passage! Wow!**

Ask:

- **After hearing 1 John 4:7-21, what do you think God thinks about love? Tell me your ideas.**

- **First John 4:9 says, "God showed how much he loved us by sending his one and only Son into the world." How does that make you feel? Explain.**

- **First John 4:11 says, "Since God loved us that much, we surely ought to love each other." How do we do that?**

Say: **Love is God's greatest gift to us, and** *we love others because God loves us.*

SEV'S STORY

Say: **God shows his love to us in many ways—even when bad things happen. Let's watch a story about a boy named Sev who found God's love through—of all things!—a horse.**

Show "Sev's Story" (track 4) from the *Grow Together Now* DVD.

Afterward ask:

- **How did God show his love for Sev and his family? Give examples.**

- **How can we show God's love to others?**

Say: **Sev and his family felt God's love through the people at Hearts and Horses. Because they felt loved, they want to share Sev's story with as many people as they can. When God shows us his love, we can do the same thing—share his love with others.** *We love others because God loves us!*

HOW DO YOU KNOW?

Give each child a half-sheet of paper and a pencil.

Say: **Pop quiz!** Allow an awkward pause... **No, just kidding, but I do want you to number from 1 to 3 on both sides of your paper. Older kids, please help younger ones with this if needed.**

Instruct children to take a few moments to think of three ways that they know God loves them—for instance, because the Bible says so or because they've seen God answer a prayer. Have them write or draw their ideas on one side of their papers. Next, have kids think of three ways that their *families and friends* know they are loved by the kids themselves. Kids can write or draw those responses on the other side of the paper.

When everyone is ready, say: **Okay, for the next 30 seconds, tell as many people as you can how you know Jesus loves you. Go!** Pause for 30 seconds; then get everyone's attention and say: **Now spend 30 seconds telling as many people as you can how your *family and friends* know they're loved by you. Ready? Go!**

Gather everyone in a circle and ask:

- **What surprised you about this little activity? Why?**

- **What would happen if no one knew you loved them? or if no one knew God loved them?**

- **What are some of the best ideas you heard today about showing love to others?**

Say: *We love others because God loves us.* **This week, let's make sure everyone we love knows about that.**

WOULD YOU RATHER...?

Have kids help you use colorful duct tape (red works great!) to mark out the letters "A" and "B" somewhere on your classroom floor. Give plenty of space between the two letters. Next use masking tape to mark out large squares around each of the duct tape letters.

Say: **We're going to play the "Would You Rather...?" game now. I'll read off a couple of choices, and you decide which choice you'd prefer. Once you decide, crowd into the square on the floor that represents your preferred choice. Ready? Here we go.**

Read from this list for the "Would You Rather...?" game, or make up new ideas of your own. Ask a few kids to explain their choices after each round.

Would You Rather...

- **(a) eat a banana dipped in mud or (b) eat a grasshopper dipped in chocolate?**

- **(a) lose your vision for a day or (b) lose your hearing for a day?**

- **(a) pray by yourself for 15 minutes or (b) listen to a crowd of other people pray for half an hour?**

- **(a) run or (b) walk?**

- **(a) go to Disney World for one weekend or (b) go to the movies every weekend for a year?**

- **(a) smear ice cream on your face or (b) squish ice cream between your toes?**

- **(a) get a new puppy or (b) get a new snake?**

- **(a) sleep on the floor or (b) sleep outside?**

- **(a) go without food for a day or (b) go without video games and TV for a day?**

- **(a) get punched in the face or (b) get a hug from someone you love?**

Afterward say: **These were silly decisions to make, but life is filled with really important decisions.** Ask:

- **What are some tough decisions kids have to make in real life?**

- **Why is it important to make wise choices?**

Say: **Our choices matter! That's why 1 John 4:7 tells us, "Dear friends, let us *continue to love one another."* That means we can *choose* to love one another, each day, in every circumstance. *We love others because God loves us.***

LIVE IT!

Say: **Jesus' friend John taught that** *we love others because God loves us.* **In fact, the letter he wrote about that is almost like a love letter to friends. Listen:**

Read aloud 1 John 4:11-21.

Next, give each child a sheet of paper, an envelope, and markers or crayons. Say: **Let's try following John's directions and example right now. Let's write a few of our own notes of love and encouragement to friends.**

Have each child write or draw an encouraging message such as "You're special" or "God loves you, and so do I," place it in an envelope, and seal the envelope. If there's time, let kids write more than one note, just for fun. When they've all sealed their envelopes, have kids trade their notes and open them.

Then lead this discussion:

- **What did you like about creating your love note for friends in this room?**

- **What went through your mind as everyone was opening notes from each other?**

- **How would you finish this sentence? "Jesus' love makes me feel like..."**

Say: *We love others because God loves us.* **Think of someone you love, and write that person a little love note to show God's love this week.**

Finish your class session with prayer, thanking God for his love and asking him to help you share that love with others during the week.

TAKE-HOME PAGE

Give each child a Take-Home page. Encourage kids to select one of the six challenges for the week ahead.

PRACTICE KINDNESS

Keep growing in your faith and character. Choose one of the following challenges to do this week.

CHALLENGE 1

Think of someone you know who might be lonely. Show God's love by inviting this person to join you for lunch or to play with you.

CHALLENGE 2

Show God's love in a quiet way by praying for a friend.

CHALLENGE 3

Do you have an enemy— someone you really don't like? God's love can help both of you. Think of one good thing about this person, and let him or her know. Who knows? It may be the start of a new friendship.

CHALLENGE 4

Send a loving note to a friend who needs encouragement, including a verse or two from the Bible.

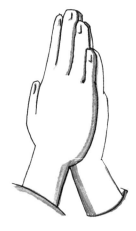

CHALLENGE 5

Pray for someone you don't really like. (I know—that's hard! But you can do it.) Ask God to give you an opportunity to show his love to that person.

CHALLENGE 6

Every day for a week, pray, "God, thank you for loving me! Help me love others because I am loved by you." Write down any experiences you have that you think might be God answering your prayer!

WE LOVE AS JESUS LOVES

LEADER PREP

Luke 23:44-49; 24:1-9

LESSON AT A GLANCE

Jesus said there isn't a greater example of love than laying down your life for your friend—and Jesus did just that. By dying on the cross, Jesus proved his love for us and connected us to God forever. Love isn't just a word; it's an action. Jesus loves us very much—we know this because he gave his life so we can live. Use this lesson to help your children learn to love as Jesus loves.

KINDNESS IS...
treating others as beloved creations of God.

WHAT KIDS DO	WHAT YOU'LL NEED
God Sightings *(5 minutes)* Talk about ways they've seen God at work.	
Explore the Bible! *(10 minutes)* Form a heart shape as they talk about Jesus' sacrificial love for us.	• Bible
Love and Tell *(15 minutes)* Practice telling others their personal stories about Jesus' kindness.	• Bible • small sports ball
Hearts and Crafts *(10 minutes)* Make a craft to keep as a symbol of how we can love like Jesus.	• half-sheets of paper *(cut vertically to form strips of paper that are 4¼x11 inches)* • markers • child-safe scissors • transparent tape • colored pencils *(optional)*
Let's Live Love *(10 minutes)* Brainstorm as many ways as possible for kids to show Jesus' love to others.	• sand timer or cellphone timer • slips of paper • pencils • hat or bowl
Live It! *(15 minutes)* Watch a video and discover how they can "pay it forward" to change another's life.	• *Grow Together Now* DVD • DVD player

ILLUSTRATED BY RONNIE ROONEY

*Photocopy the Take-Home page at the end of this lesson for each child.

53

DEVOTIONS FOR LEADERS:

KINDNESS

Today you'll share with your kids the central belief of the Christian faith: Jesus' resurrection. The resurrection changes everything. Not only can Jesus be our friend, but if we ask, he can be our forever friend. Beyond the kids in your class, who in your life needs Jesus' love? And how can you share that love this week? Ask God to show you someone who needs his love. Decide now that you'll be open for God to use you in telling that person your faith story. Because that's what friends do.

BIBLE BACKGROUND FOR LEADERS

Luke 23:44-49; 24:1-9: Jesus Dies for His Friends

NO GREATER LOVE

About noon, as Jesus was dying on the cross, an eerie darkness blanketed the area. In the Temple, the veil shielding the holy of holies (the inner chamber of the sanctuary in the Temple in Jerusalem) split, torn from top to bottom. The timing wasn't a coincidence. A short distance away, Jesus slumped lower on the cross, gasped, "It is finished," and gave up his spirit (John 19:30). In Greek, one possible meaning of the word Jesus uttered, *tetelestai*, translates "paid in full." The Roman soldier supervising the crucifixion marveled, "Surely this man was innocent."

Jesus' friends stood helplessly nearby and soon sadly made their way home. They misunderstood what they had witnessed. They thought Jesus was a victim, but in reality, he was the victor. He'd given his life for them and the rest of humanity, living out earlier words: "There is no greater love than to lay down one's life for one's friends" (John 15:13).

MOURNING FRIENDS

Three days later, several of Jesus' friends went to his tomb. They came to anoint Jesus' body with spices and ointments and then wrap it in linen strips. After several years, decay would reduce Jesus' body to bare bones, and they would come back to place the bones in a small stone box known as an ossuary. Their care would continue, even after Jesus' death. That's what friends did for each other in that day.

ILLUSTRATED BY PAMELA JOHNSON

ANGELIC EYE-OPENER

Upon their arrival at the tomb, the women found the large entrance stone rolled away and Jesus' body gone. Grave robbers? They ducked into the tomb to search. As they tried to piece together what had happened, two angels appeared. Clothed in dazzling robes, the angels conveyed an even more dazzling reminder: Jesus' prediction of his death and resurrection. "Why are you looking among the dead for someone who is alive?" they asked. Jesus had died for his friends—and for us—because he loves us so dearly.

THE LESSON

GOD SIGHTINGS

Use the text below or substitute your own examples for this weekly lesson-starter activity.

Say: **James 1:17 in the Bible reminds us that "Whatever is good and perfect is a gift coming down to us from God our Father." That means the gift of a beautiful sunset is evidence of God. When your friend shares with you, that's God's kindness at work. When you smile at others or hold open a door, you're showing God's joy.**

It's important that we recognize and thank God for the ways we see him all around us and the ways he is at work in our lives. We call these God Sightings.

Ask: **How have you seen God at work this week? What evidence have you seen of God's creativity, joy, forgiveness, and goodness?**

Think about God's creation, ways people have encouraged you, and even ways God helped you make a difference for someone else.

As a group, share God Sightings. Then celebrate God's gifts in your lives with a prayer of thanksgiving.

✓ **Bible**

EXPLORE THE BIBLE!

Open this activity with a question: **What's the most amazing thing a friend has ever done for you? Tell about it.** Tell an example from your own life; then let kids share.

Allow time for a few kids to respond, and then say: **John 15:13 tells us that "There is no greater love than to lay down one's life for one's friends." And guess what! That's exactly what Jesus did. Jesus loved his friends so much that he was willing to die for them—and for us too. Amazing! Let's read about what happened.**

Read aloud Luke 23:44-49; 24:1-9.

Say: **Let's do something unusual while we talk more about this. It's an activity called "Heart and Soles," because we are going to lie on the floor, head to toe, and see if we can form ourselves into the shape of a heart.**

Have kids lie on the floor and form a heart shape using their bodies. (See the diagram on this page for help on what that looks like.) If your class size is larger, it's okay if you have to make several smaller hearts instead of one large heart on the floor.

While kids are in the shape of a heart, lead this discussion:

- **What does it mean that Jesus laid down his life for us?**

- **You and I obviously aren't going to be crucified anytime soon, so what do you think it means for us to lay down *our* lives for others?**

Have kids return to their seats. Say: **Just as you physically lay down in the shape of a heart, Jesus took action and physically gave up his life by dying on the cross for our sins. The good news is that we don't have to die on a cross today! But when *we love as Jesus loves*, we're following his example of being the most amazing friend ever.**

LOVE AND TELL

YOU'LL NEED:

✓ **Bible**

✓ **small sports ball**

Say: **After Jesus died and then came back to life, his friends were so excited! Let's read about what they did.** Read aloud Acts 4:1-14.

Say: **Like Peter and John, one very important way *we love as Jesus loves* is by being kind enough to tell others what happened—so they can become friends with Jesus too.**

Have kids form a circle, sitting at arm's length from each other.

Say: **Let's practice that sort of kindness right now. We'll toss a ball around. When I say "stop," the person holding the ball will get to tell us all a true story about Jesus in his or her life.**

Use the following prompts as the ball is tossed:

- **Talk about a time you were scared but Jesus was with you.**

- **Talk about why you love Jesus.**

- **Talk about a time Jesus helped you with something.**

- **Talk about why you believe in Jesus.**

- **Talk about what Jesus did while he was on earth.**

- **Talk about how you know Jesus is alive.**

Play several rounds. Then lead this discussion:

- **What was it like for you just now, when you told your friends about your experience with Jesus?**

- **Why is it a kind act for us to tell others about Jesus? Explain your thinking.**

- **Some people don't like to hear about Jesus. How can we be kind to them without hiding who we are as Jesus' friends?**

Finish this activity by asking kids: **Who told you about Jesus?** Then lead a cheer for all those people who shared about God with your kids.

✓ **half-sheets of paper**
(cut vertically to form
strips of paper that are
4¼x11 inches)

✓ **markers**

✓ **child-safe scissors**

✓ **transparent tape**

✓ **colored pencils**
(optional)

HEARTS AND CRAFTS

Say: **Let's make a craft to keep as a symbol of how *we love*
*as Jesus loves.***

Give each child a half-sheet of paper (cut vertically so that each
strip of paper is 4¼x11 inches), and a marker. Make available
child-safe scissors for kids to share with others nearby. Then have
children follow these steps:

1. Fold a strip of paper accordion-style with eight even sections.
   (See the diagram below for reference.)

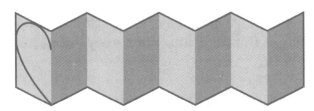

2. Use a marker to draw half of a heart shape on the top of the
   accordion, with the inside of the heart touching the folded
   edge and the rounded part touching the top and side edges as
   shown in the illustration. (See diagram.)

3. Cut along the lines, but not where the heart touches the folded
   edge of the paper.

4. Unfold the paper to reveal a strip of four hearts.

5. Tape the two ends together to make a loop.

After everyone is finished, ask:

- **How did this craft surprise you?**

- **Why do you think this craft can be a good symbol to**
  remind us that *we love as Jesus loves?*

If time allows, set out colored pencils and let children decorate
their hearts.

LET'S LIVE LOVE

Say: *We love as Jesus loves us*—but how do we show that in real life? Let's try this brainstorming game to help us think of lots of ways to love others.

Have kids form groups of up to three people, and number each group to create teams. Give each team several slips of paper and pencils. Tell kids to write their team number on all the papers they have.

Next, place a hat (or a bowl) where everyone can see it and can reach it easily. Pull out a timer (a sand timer if you're "old school" or the timer on your cellphone if you're "new school") and show it to the class.

Say: **I'm going to read off a list of people and places. Every time I read something from the list, I'll reset my timer to 30 seconds. In your team, quickly brainstorm ideas for how we might show God's love to those people or in that place. Try to make your ideas as specific to that person or place as possible. Write every new idea on a slip of paper, and then have someone run up and place it in the hat. Be sure every slip of paper has your team number on it somewhere. Keep doing that until time runs out for each round. Ready? Let's go!**

Read from the list below and start timing.

1. **Church**
2. **Neighborhood**
3. **Family**
4. **Grandparents**
5. **Brothers or Sisters**
6. **Friend**
7. **Coach**
8. **Teachers**

After kids have brainstormed a word for 30 seconds, pull slips out of the hat and read the ideas. See how many unique ideas your group came up with. Play as many rounds as time allows.

YOU'LL NEED:

✓ **sand timer or cellphone timer**
✓ **slips of paper**
✓ **pencils**
✓ **hat or bowl**

Then ask:

- **Why do you think God wants us to always be thinking of ways we can show love to others?**

- **What should we do with all these great ideas we've brainstormed?**

Encourage kids to try out a few ideas at home this week.

LIVE IT!

Lead kids in this discussion:

- **Tell about a time someone did a small act of kindness for you or your family. What happened?** Tell an example from your own life; then have kids share.

- **Why do small acts of kindness matter?**

- **How do acts of kindness show Jesus' love to others?**

Say: **When *we love as Jesus loves*, sometimes the smallest act of kindness can make a really big difference. As our closing today, I want to have you watch a video that'll show you what I mean.**

Show "Pay It Forward" (track 5) from the *Grow Together Now* DVD.

Afterward, encourage your kids to perform a small act of kindness for someone in their family this week. Then close your class session with prayer.

TAKE-HOME PAGE

Give each child a Take-Home page. Encourage kids to select one of the six challenges for the week ahead.

PRACTICE KINDNESS

Keep growing in your faith and character. Choose one of the following challenges to do this week.

CHALLENGE 1

Look for hearts as a reminder that Jesus loves you.

CHALLENGE 2

Find one way you can share Jesus' love with someone else by helping that person.

CHALLENGE 3

Write down one thing that happened during the day that made you realize Jesus loves you.

CHALLENGE 4

Read 1 John 4:7-12. Thank God for loving you so much that he sent his only Son, Jesus, to die for you. Then say a prayer of commitment, promising God to love your friends deeply.

CHALLENGE 5

Draw the outline of a cross, and put it somewhere in your room. Every time you do something loving for a friend, draw a heart inside the cross.

CHALLENGE 6

Every day for a week, pray, "God, show me how to love others well—just like you do." Write down any experiences you have that you think might be God answering your prayer!

GOD WANTS US TO BE KIND TO OTHERS

LEADER PREP

Ruth 1

LESSON AT A GLANCE

After Naomi lost her husband and sons, she headed back to her home a sad and broken woman. Ruth, Naomi's daughter-in-law, showed kindness by staying with Naomi and refusing to leave her. God will send the Holy Spirit to help us be kind, too. Use this lesson to help your children learn that God wants us to be kind to others.

KINDNESS IS... treating others as beloved creations of God.

ILLUSTRATED BY PAMELA JOHNSON

WHAT KIDS DO	WHAT YOU'LL NEED
God Sightings *(5 minutes)* Talk about ways they've seen God at work.	
Explore the Bible! *(10 minutes)* Practice "kind-sight" as a way of discovering a Scripture story.	• Bible
Museum of Kindness *(15 minutes)* Pretend to work in a museum that's looking for ways to be kind.	• 4 to 6 "everyday objects" *(such as a hammer, crayons, a plate, a child's toy, and a picture book)*
The Praying Kind *(10 minutes)* Draw sketches and use them as prompts for prayer.	• 3x5 cards • pencils
X-Game *(10 minutes)* Toss pennies toward a target, and discuss how to overcome obstacles to kindness.	• Bible • 1 penny per child • colorful duct tape
Live It! *(15 minutes)* Help each other think of creative ways to show kindness every day.	

*Photocopy the Take-Home page at the end of this lesson for each child.

DEVOTIONS FOR LEADERS:

KINDNESS

What hurting person can you encourage? Where is a stranger you can help? Which enemy can you choose to care for? Invite God to point you toward a specific opportunity to perform an act of kindness today.

BIBLE BACKGROUND FOR LEADERS

Ruth 1: Ruth Is Kind to Naomi

ONE FOOT IN FRONT OF THE OTHER

Ruth and her sister-in-law, Orpah, found themselves in a painful and scary situation. Both their husbands had died; in a culture in which women generally weren't able to earn money, the two young widows had no means of survival. To make matters worse, their father-in-law had also died, leaving their mother-in-law, Naomi, widowed as well.

Naomi urged Ruth and Orpah to do the only logical thing: return to their families in Moab, while Naomi traveled back to her home in Judah. Orpah, through tears, hugged her mother-in-law goodbye and headed for home. Ruth could have followed suit but instead made a choice of extreme kindness. With no plan for survival and completely dependent upon the charity of others, Ruth journeyed with her mother-in-law to a foreign land.

KINDNESS IS A CHOICE

The Bible calls us to be kind—and sometimes it's not an easy choice. No one showed kindness better than Jesus. Jesus chose, oftentimes against cultural norms, to serve others with kindness. We're called to this same, self-sacrificing type of kindness—to make kind choices that may be hard. Jesus asks us to treat others with more than smiley-face politeness. He calls us to feed, clothe, and care for strangers (Matthew 25:31-46), to show lovingkindness even to those people who rub us the wrong way (Matthew 5:43-48).

ASKING MORE

We can "follow the Spirit's leading in every part of our lives" (Galatians 5:25), and that's particularly true when it comes to choices that express kindness. God's Spirit nudges us in moments

ILLUSTRATED BY PAIGE BILLIN-FRYE

when we can choose either our own comfort or caring for others. He challenges us to step out into situations that may not be comfortable. Imagine how Ruth felt! You may feel a sense of risk as you take steps of kindness—that's a good thing! In those moments, we realize how dependent we are on the Spirit.

THE LESSON

GOD SIGHTINGS

Use the text below or substitute your own examples for this weekly lesson-starter activity.

Say: **James 1:17 in the Bible reminds us that "Whatever is good and perfect is a gift coming down to us from God our Father." That means the gift of a beautiful sunset is evidence of God. When your friend shares with you, that's God's kindness at work. When you smile at others or hold open a door, you're showing God's joy.**

It's important that we recognize and thank God for the ways we see him all around us and the ways he is at work in our lives. We call these God Sightings.

Ask: **How have you seen God at work this week? What evidence have you seen of God's creativity, joy, forgiveness, and goodness?**

Think about God's creation, ways people have encouraged you, and even ways God helped you make a difference for someone else.

As a group, share God Sightings. Then celebrate God's gifts in your lives with a prayer of thanksgiving.

EXPLORE THE BIBLE!

Say: *God wants us to be kind to others,* **so to start off our Bible lesson today we're going to practice something I call "kind-sight." I'm going to read a true story from Ruth chapter 1. It's about a woman named Naomi and her two daughters-in-law, Ruth and Orpah. As I read, I want you to be looking and listening for moments when someone**

YOU'LL NEED:

✓ **Bible**

is kind. When you think someone is being kind, stand up, interrupt my reading, and tell me why. Ready?

Read Ruth 1 aloud, allowing moments for kids to interrupt and tell you why they think Ruth, Naomi, or Orpah is being kind. Speak encouragingly to kids who have good "kind-sight" about noticing kindnesses in the Scripture.

Afterward ask:

- **What do you notice most about the people in this passage from the Bible?**

- **How did kindness reflect their love for each other?**

Say: **Your kindness interrupted me—it made me stop and listen.** Ask:

- **In real life, how do acts of kindness sometimes stop you or surprise you?**

- **Think about your past week. When was someone kind to you?** Tell your own story; then have kids share their own accounts.

Say: **In the Bible, Ruth's kindness changed Naomi's life! When people are kind, it's sometimes a surprise—something we don't expect. Let's explore more about the way kindness changes us.**

MUSEUM OF KINDNESS

Talk about: *God wants us to be kind to others,* **and there are lots of ways we can do that in our everyday lives. We can offer a kind word, hold the door open for someone, or even share a simple smile!**

Display your everyday objects so all the children can see them.

Say: **I have a challenge for you now. Let's imagine we live in the future and work for the Museum of Kindness. These objects are all on display in that museum, but nobody remembers how people used them to be kind to each other. Our job, then, is to figure out creative ways people could use our objects to show kindness to others. We have three minutes—let's work in pairs and see how many ideas we can come up with!**

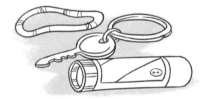

YOU'LL NEED:

✓ **4 to 6 "everyday objects"** *(such as a hammer, crayons, a plate, a child's toy, and a picture book)*

Have children form pairs and take three minutes brainstorming ideas. If time allows, have pairs join together to create foursomes, and spend two more minutes letting kids share ideas with each other. Then have kids tell a few of their best ideas to the whole group.

Afterward lead this discussion:

- **Some people think it's too hard to always be kind to others. Now that you've been to the Museum of Kindness, what would you say to those people?**

- **What are other things you might use to show kindness to someone?**

- **What do you think would happen if everybody you know was kind to one another?**

Say: **There are some objects, like the ones in our museum, that are around us all the time. *God wants us to be kind to others*, and we can use those objects—and lots of other things—to show his kindness every day.**

THE PRAYING KIND

Say: **One of the best ways to be kind to someone else is simply to pray for that person. And we can pray anytime— even right in the middle of a Bible lesson! *God wants us to be kind to others*, so let's practice praying for people right this minute.**

Give every child a 3x5 card and a pencil. Say: **Think of one person you'd like to pray for right now. It might be a parent, a friend, your brother or sister, a leader at church, or anyone else that comes to mind. Draw a little sketch of that person on your card.**

Tell kids to follow your prompts as you lead them in praying for the people on their cards. Pause for at least 30 seconds between prompts.

- **Let's pray that God will show his love in a special way to the person on your card. How do you think God might do that? Ask him about it, and tell him your thoughts.**

- **Let's pray for your person's well-being. What might help that person feel healthy and strong? Talk to God about that.**

- Let's pray for your person's worries. What do you think that person is worried about, scared about, or concerned about? Ask God to help in those areas.

- Let's pray for your person's work or school. Ask God to bring success and joy in those places.

- Let's thank God for this person in your life. Tell God why you are thankful to know him or her!

Say: **Amen! Fold your card and put it in your pocket. Keep it nearby this week to help you remember that** *God wants us to be kind to others*—**and we can always be kind in prayer.**

X-GAME

Read Ruth 1:15-16 aloud.

Say: **Ruth, Naomi's daughter-in-law, showed kindness by staying with Naomi and refusing to leave her. That was a hard choice! Ruth had to leave her home, but she was kind even when it was hard.**

Ask: **When is it hard for you to be kind?** Tell an example from your own life before kids share.

Say: **Let's play a game to explore more about this.**

Use brightly colored duct tape to mark a large "X" on the floor. (Red usually works well for this activity, but any color will do.) Have kids stand in a line about 6 feet away from the X. Give every child a penny.

Say: **How good are you at hitting a target? Flick your penny into the air and see if you can make it land on the X. Ready? Go!**

Have kids retrieve a penny (any one will do) and repeat the game. Play for several rounds; then gather all kids into a circle for discussion. Ask:

- **What made it hard or easy to hit the X every time?**

- **What makes it hard for you to hit God's goal of being kind to others?**

YOU'LL NEED:

✓ **Bible**

✓ **1 penny per child**

✓ **colorful duct tape**

- **What can we do to help when it feels hard to be kind to someone else?**

Say: **Just as it can be hard to hit a target from far away, it can be hard to always be kind. But** *God wants us to be kind to others,* **and if we try to do that every day, he will help us succeed.**

LIVE IT!

Assign the following themes to different walls of your classroom:

- Family

- Friends

- Others

Say: *God wants us to be kind to others*—**and we can do that every day this week if we try! Let's brainstorm ideas to help us know what to do.**

Have kids gather in front of the "Family" wall. Encourage children to shout out ideas for ways they might show kindness to a family member during the upcoming week. Then have the group repeat the process for the "Friends" and "Others" walls.

Afterward, say: **Those are some pretty great ideas! Let's plan to do at least one idea from each wall during the next week. You can tell me how it goes next time we meet!**

Close this session with a prayer, thanking God for his kindness and asking him to help your kids complete their ideas in the coming week.

TAKE-HOME PAGE

Give each child a Take-Home page. Encourage kids to select one of the six challenges for the week ahead.

PRACTICE KINDNESS

Keep growing in your faith and character. Choose one of the following challenges to do this week.

CHALLENGE 1

Pick a friend, and secretly do something kind for that person. You could make a snack and leave it out for the person, write the person a nice card, or do anything else you think of.

CHALLENGE 2

With your parents' supervision, offer to pet-sit or be a dog-walker for a neighbor. You'll help your neighbor—and get to hang out with a dog too. Yay!

CHALLENGE 3

Be especially kind to your mom or dad. Tell your parent why you love and appreciate him or her. Then give your parent a big hug. Explain that just as Ruth was kind to Naomi, God wants us to be kind to others through our words and actions.

CHALLENGE 4

Show kindness to a younger sibling this week. Let your brother or sister tag along with you and your friends, or allow your sibling to play with one of your favorite toys. Tell your brother or sister how God wants us to be kind to others.

CHALLENGE 5

Look up the following Bible verses about God's kindness to us: Ephesians 4:32; Romans 2:4; and Psalm 116:5. Think about one way you can imitate God's kindness to someone in your family today. Then do it!

CHALLENGE 6

Every day for a week, pray, "God, show me how to be truly kind to others today." Write down any experiences you have that you think might be God answering your prayer!

WE SHOW GOD'S KINDNESS BY ENCOURAGING EACH OTHER

LEADER PREP

Genesis 37:3-36

LESSON AT A GLANCE

Joseph's father gave him a beautiful coat as a gesture of love and encouragement. Unfortunately, Joseph's brothers were jealous because of the gift, and they treated Joseph badly. Unlike Joseph's brothers, we encourage the people around us. Use this lesson to help your children learn that they can show God's love by encouraging each other.

KINDNESS IS...
treating others as beloved creations of God.

WHAT KIDS DO	WHAT YOU'LL NEED
God Sightings *(5 minutes)* Talk about ways they've seen God at work.	
Explore the Bible! *(10 minutes)* Act out ways Joseph and his brothers could have made better choices.	• Bible
It Really Happened *(15 minutes)* Play a game that helps kids remember when others have encouraged them.	• 3 chairs
My Little Brother *(10 minutes)* Watch a video and discuss what to do when we fall short of God's goal.	• *Grow Together Now* DVD • DVD player
The Wall *(10 minutes)* Help overcome a wall of obstacles that might prevent encouraging acts.	• paper • marker • transparent tape
Live It! *(15 minutes)* Prepare to encourage friends and family with God's promise in Scripture.	• photocopies of the "God's Promises" handout, 1 per child • pencils • child-safe scissors

*Photocopy the Take-Home page at the end of this lesson for each child.

ILLUSTRATED BY RONNIE ROONEY

DEVOTIONS FOR LEADERS:

KINDNESS

Have jealousy and anger caused a rift in your household? When family members are angry at each other or jealous of one another's accomplishments, they're not encouraging one another as God commands. A family that encourages one another daily instead of cutting each other down will be stronger and happier, as well as obedient to God. Choose words that will build up the confidence of your family members—words that show love and acceptance. Show family members that when they encourage each other instead of nurturing strife and jealousy, they're creating harmonious and loving relationships.

BIBLE BACKGROUND FOR LEADERS

Genesis 37:3-36: Joseph Is Sold Into Slavery

JOSEPH'S JEALOUS BROTHERS

Most have heard the story of the coat of many colors, but not all remember the trouble that coat caused. Jacob loved Joseph more than his other sons because Joseph had been born to him in his old age and Rachel, Jacob's most loved wife, carried him. The richly ornamented robe further intensified the brothers' feelings of jealousy. They hated Joseph because he was so clearly their father's favorite. The situation worsened when Joseph told his brothers about the dreams he had where his brothers bowed down to him.

A DESPERATE PLAN

It seems Jacob may have been blissfully unaware of Joseph's brothers' hatred. So Jacob asked Joseph to go check on his brothers as they tended the flocks at Shechem. Jacob seemed to have no idea of the situation he was sending his favorite son into. When Joseph's brothers saw him coming, all their anger and jealousy seemed to reach a boiling point. They plotted among themselves, wanting to kill him. Reuben, the oldest brother, showed concern for Joseph's life. His idea to put Joseph in a cistern (probably a dry well) in the desert may not have been enthusiastically supported by his brothers, but they followed along anyway. Reuben's secret plan was to eventually rescue Joseph from the cistern and return him to his father.

ILLUSTRATED BY PAIGE BILLIN-FRYE

JOSEPH IS SOLD AS A SLAVE

When Ishmaelite traders came along, Judah suddenly suggested they spare Joseph's life. We don't know if this suggestion was prompted by pangs of guilt, the appeal of money, or a desire to punish Joseph even more severely by making a slave of him. Whatever the motive, Joseph was gone before Reuben returned. Then the brothers deceived their father into thinking that Joseph had been torn apart by a wild animal. In reality, Joseph became a slave to Potiphar, an officer in Pharaoh's household.

THE ULTIMATE LESSON

Although God eventually reconciled this family, the story serves as a model of how jealousy and anger dissolves family bonds. None of the members of this family really loved each other in God's way. To honor God, family members must show God's love to one another. No matter what or who the problem is within our families, God wants us to love our families with the same love he shows for us.

THE LESSON

GOD SIGHTINGS

Use the text below or substitute your own examples for this weekly lesson-starter activity.

Say: **James 1:17 in the Bible reminds us that "Whatever is good and perfect is a gift coming down to us from God our Father." That means the gift of a beautiful sunset is evidence of God. When your friend shares with you, that's God's kindness at work. When you smile at others or hold open a door, you're showing God's joy.**

It's important that we recognize and thank God for the ways we see him all around us and the ways he is at work in our lives. We call these God Sightings.

Ask: **How have you seen God at work this week? What evidence have you seen of God's creativity, joy, forgiveness, and goodness?**

Think about God's creation, ways people have encouraged you, and even ways God helped you make a difference for someone else.

As a group, share God Sightings—ways you've each seen God at work. Then celebrate God's gifts in your lives with a prayer of thanksgiving.

EXPLORE THE BIBLE!

Say: **Today we're going to explore an event from the life of a guy in the Bible, named Joseph. Through Joseph's life, we'll learn how** *we show God's kindness by encouraging each other.* **To start, let's read Genesis 37:3-36 in the Bible. As I read, listen for times people could do something different to be encouraging instead of hurtful.**

Invite four volunteers to come up front to help as you read the Scripture with drama and enthusiasm. (Because this is a longer passage, it's a good idea to use a kid-friendly Bible translation.) Have one play the part of Joseph and the rest play his brothers. Tell them to creatively act out what happens as you read the Bible passage.

Afterward, thank your volunteers. Then ask the class:

- **What are your first thoughts after hearing this story?**

- **What are some ways people could have been encouraging instead of hurtful in this situation?**

Say: **Let's see what happens if Joseph had been able to "Take 2" on this situation!**

Call up your volunteers again, and reread the Bible passage. At moments when people are hurtful in the Scriptural account, stop reading and ask kids for a "Take 2"—an idea of what Joseph or his brothers could have done to be encouraging instead of hurtful. Have your volunteers act out the "Take 2" for the class.

Afterward, say: **Following your ideas would've been a lot better for Joseph and his brothers! Unfortunately, we can't always "Take 2" in real life.**

Ask:

- **Why do you think it's so important for us to choose to encourage each other?**

- **What are a few creative ways we might be encouraging at home? at church? at school?**

Say: **Joseph and his brothers are a good example for us...
an example of what *not* to do! Instead of being unkind
like them, let's remember that *we show God's kindness by
encouraging each other.***

IT REALLY HAPPENED!

Have kids form groups of no more than three people. Say: **Let's
play the game "It Really Happened!" In your group, tell
each other a true story of a time you felt sad and someone
did something that encouraged you.** Give your own example
to get kids thinking. Pause while kids have group discussion.

When kids are ready, say: **Now, as a group, *make up* a story
about the same kind of thing—but it's something that
didn't really happen. In a minute we're going to see if
people can guess which of your stories really happened
and which one is the made-up story.**

Give kids a moment to make up a story. Then set three chairs
up front. Invite one of the groups to come up and fill the chairs,
and have each of those children tell one of their stories—two
kids telling true stories, and one telling the made-up story. After
hearing the stories, let the class shout "It really happened!" to
vote for stories they think are true, and see if they get them right.
Repeat with other groups as time allows.

Afterward say: **Some of our stories were made-up, but so
many of these encouraging stories "really happened!"
God has shown each one of us kindness by having others
encourage us. Likewise, *we show God's kindness by
encouraging each other.***

MY LITTLE BROTHER

Talk about this: ***We show God's kindness by encouraging each
other*, but sometimes we fall short. Do you ever tease or
make fun of your brother or sister?** Pause. **Do you ever
fight or have trouble playing nicely together?** Pause. **Joseph
and his brothers struggled with those kinds of things, too.
Let's watch a story about them.**

Show "My Little Brother" (track 6) from the *Grow
Together Now* DVD.

Afterward, lead this discussion:

- **What do you think of the way Joseph's brothers treated him?**

- **Can you think of a time a brother, sister, or friend treated you poorly? Tell someone next to you about that.** Pause for discussion.

- **What are two things you could do to be kind when it feels like someone is treating you poorly? Tell your ideas to the person next to you.**

Say: **Joseph's brothers forgot that** *we show God's kindness by encouraging each other.* **Let's not make that same mistake this week!**

THE WALL

Say: **We know that** *we show God's kindness by encouraging each other,* **but sometimes it feels hard to do that.**

Invite a volunteer to stand by you. Ask: **What kinds of things might get in my way and keep me from choosing to encourage** [volunteer's name]**?**

Have kids brainstorm ideas in answer to the question. Write one of the ideas on a sheet of paper. Invite another volunteer to the front, and tape that paper to that second volunteer. That person is now an "Obstacle." Place the Obstacle person between you and the first child. Repeat two or three times until there's a "wall" of Obstacle people between you and the original volunteer.

Say: **Oh no! Now there's a wall of obstacles between me and** [volunteer's name]**. The wall is keeping me from encouraging** [volunteer's name]**.**

Ask: **What could I do to help me overcome the obstacles in this wall?**

Have kids brainstorm new ideas in answer to the question. As they brainstorm, write some of their ideas on new sheets of paper. Tape the new ideas over the top of the old ones, until there are no more "obstacles" left.

YOU'LL NEED:

✓ **paper**

✓ **marker**

✓ **transparent tape**

FOR LEADERS:

If there are fewer than eight children in your class, use chairs to build your "wall" instead of volunteers.

Say: **These are great ideas! Let's try to remember them next time we have an opportunity to encourage and be kind to others.**

LIVE IT!

Have older children help younger ones in this activity.

Say: **One really cool way to encourage others is to remind them of God's special promises from the Bible.**

Form pairs, and give each child a copy of the "God's Promises" handout. Invite partners to read the Scriptures on the handout aloud to each other.

Then say: **There are three Scriptures on your paper. One is for you, and the other two are for people you want to encourage. Write your name on one Scripture you'd like to keep and names of other people you'd like to encourage on each of the other two.**

When kids are ready, give scissors to each pair and have them cut their handouts into thirds so each Scripture is separate from the others. Tell kids to fold up the Scripture they will keep and put it in a pocket. Encourage them to take the other two Scriptures home and to deliver them to their chosen people sometime during the week.

Say: *We show God's kindness by encouraging each other.* **Let's ask Jesus to help us do that well this week.**

Close your class session with a prayer, thanking God for his promises and asking Jesus to help you all be encouragers this week.

TAKE-HOME PAGE

Give each child a Take-Home page. Encourage kids to select one of the six challenges for the week ahead.

YOU'LL NEED:

✓ **photocopies of the "God's Promises" handout, 1 per child**

✓ **pencils**

✓ **child-safe scissors**

PRACTICE KINDNESS

Keep growing in your faith and character. Choose one of the following challenges to do this week.

CHALLENGE 1

Give a brother, sister, or friend an "encouragement balloon." Inflate a balloon, write "You're the Best!" on it, and decorate the balloon however you want. When you give the balloon away, tell the person one thing about him or her that you're thankful for.

CHALLENGE 2

Think of a friend who has seemed down or discouraged about something. Make a special point to think of and share encouraging words with that person today.

CHALLENGE 3

Share something encouraging with each of your family members. Keep a small piece of paper in your pocket and fold it in half each time you catch yourself encouraging one of them—fold it until it won't fold anymore.

CHALLENGE 4

Make a gift for a sibling (or a friend) who you've noticed is doing really well at something. Make a card, some cookies, or a trophy to recognize the person's talent. Give it to that person as an expression of love, and share why you chose to give it to him or her.

CHALLENGE 5

Read Genesis 37:3-36. Rewrite the story, including what the brothers could've done to show God's love by encouraging Joseph.

CHALLENGE 6

Every day for a week, pray, "God, help me to see new opportunities to show your kindness by encouraging others." Write down any experiences you have that you think might be God answering your prayer!

GOD'S PROMISES

JOSHUA 1:9

"Do not be afraid or discouraged. For the Lord your God is with you wherever you go."

PSALM 32:8

"The Lord says, 'I will guide you along the best pathway for your life.' "

ROMANS 8:28

"God causes everything to work together for the good of those who love God."

WE SHOW GOD'S KINDNESS TO THE WORLD

LEADER PREP

Matthew 5:13-16

LESSON AT A GLANCE

Jesus tells his followers to be the salt of the earth and the light of the world. In Jesus' time, people used salt for preventing meat from decaying quickly, so it was essential. The good deeds we do and the kind things we say give the world flavor and preserve it from moral decay. Jesus also calls us to shine his light and show God's love to the world by the good deeds and kind things we do. Use this lesson to teach kids that Jesus' example was about showing, not just telling, the world about God's love.

KINDNESS IS...
treating others as beloved creations of God.

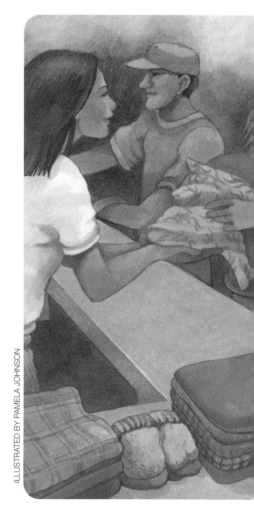

ILLUSTRATED BY PAMELA JOHNSON

WHAT KIDS DO	WHAT YOU'LL NEED
God Sightings *(5 minutes)* Talk about ways they've seen God at work.	
Explore the Bible! *(10 minutes)* Watch a video about showing love, and explore how to do that in their lives.	• Bible • *Grow Together Now* DVD • DVD player
Light Force *(15 minutes)* Play a game to discover more about what it means to shine God's light in the world.	• plain white paper plates • markers • worship music
Ask/Answer *(10 minutes)* Ask any questions they have about Matthew 5:13-16.	• Bibles • 3x5 cards • pencils
Sit/Stand *(10 minutes)* Play a game that helps them discover how to shine good deeds in their world.	
Live It! *(15 minutes)* Draw "finger-candles" as reminders to be God's light in the world this week.	• washable markers

*Photocopy the Take-Home page at the end of this lesson for each child.

81

DEVOTIONS FOR LEADERS:

KINDNESS

Though inspiring, Jesus' words here aren't a mere feel-good message. They don't let us pat ourselves on the back and say, "I'm so great!" Rather, Jesus' words compel us to face ourselves in a mirror, to ask, "Have I lost my saltiness?" and "Is my light shining brightly...or is it hidden away?" Are we living as the world lives, or are we living differently, in a way that calls others to sit up and pay attention to God's values? Do we shine the inviting light of God's love?

BIBLE BACKGROUND FOR LEADERS

Matthew 5:13-16: Light of the World

CALLED TO BE DIFFERENT

Jesus had just finished describing God's values in Matthew 5:3-12, calling his followers to be merciful, pure, and humble peacemakers—in other words, to live radically differently from the way the world called them to live. In response to those words, it's tempting to think that we should pull away from the world and hide out, living by Jesus' values in our own safe little Christian communities. But the very next words Jesus said called people to do exactly the opposite: not only to live in this world but to powerfully influence it.

PASS THE SALT

Jesus called his followers "the salt of the earth." In Jesus' time, salt had much more than dinner-table, flavor-enhancer status. Salt was an extremely valuable commodity—in fact, Roman soldiers received a *salarium* (from which we get the word *salary*), a monetary allotment for buying salt. Without salt, a piece of meat would quickly go bad, becoming unsafe to eat and eventually completely decaying. In Jesus' word picture, salt preserves the world. Jesus told his followers that they were valuable and even essential to preserving God's morality in the world; without such "salt," moral decay is inevitable.

OUR LIGHT SOURCE

Jesus also proclaimed, "You are the light of the world." In a world without electric streetlights, a city of brightly lit homes could

ILLUSTRATED BY PAIGE BILLIN-FRYE

easily be seen from afar on a dark night. It would be a beacon of hope, a guiding landmark, and a destination for travelers. This is the picture Jesus paints of Christian faith.

This isn't the only time Jesus used the phrase "light of the world"; he also said, "I am the light of the world" (John 8:12; 9:5). The psalmist David once wrote, "In your light we see light" (Psalm 36:9, NIV). God is the light that illuminates us, that enables us to know truth and experience peace and joy and love. When Jesus' light fills us, that light can shine through us into a dark world.

ACTIONS THAT SHINE

It's not just being a Christian or believing in Jesus that somehow fills us with light. Jesus made clear that the light shines as we "let [our] good deeds shine out for all to see." It's our actions that shine brilliantly, pointing others to God. We show God's kindness to the world through our own loving, light-filled choices.

THE LESSON

GOD SIGHTINGS

Use the text below or substitute your own examples for this weekly lesson-starter activity.

Say: **James 1:17 in the Bible reminds us that "Whatever is good and perfect is a gift coming down to us from God our Father." That means the gift of a beautiful sunset is evidence of God. When your friend shares with you, that's God's kindness at work. When you smile at others or hold open a door, you're showing God's joy.**

It's important that we recognize and thank God for the ways we see him all around us and the ways he is at work in our lives. We call these God Sightings.

Ask: **How have you seen God at work this week? What evidence have you seen of God's creativity, joy, forgiveness, and goodness?**

Think about God's creation, ways people have encouraged you, and even ways God helped you make a difference for someone else.

As a group, share God Sightings—ways you've each seen God at work. Then celebrate God's gifts in your lives with a prayer of thanksgiving.

EXPLORE THE BIBLE!

Start by asking kids to discuss these questions:

- **What do you know about light? Educate me!**

- **What are a few specific activities that need light? What happens if we try to do those things in the dark?**

Say: **Today we're exploring how Jesus wants *us* to be his light to those around us. That means when *we show God's kindness to the world*, we're helping people find their way to God. Jesus talked about this in the Bible—let's read that right now.**

Read aloud Matthew 5:13-16.

Say: **We know that *we show God's kindness to the world*. But have you really stopped to think about what that looks like? The singers in a music video did. They randomly stopped people on the street and asked them about the true meaning of Christmas and who the light of the world is. Let's see what happened.**

Show "Showing Love" (track 7) from the *Grow Together Now* DVD.

Afterward, lead this discussion:

- **What's one thing you heard in the video about showing God's love that you'd like to remember? Why?**

- **If someone watched you for a day, what would that person learn about God's love?**

Say: **We show God's kindness to the world through our actions and our attitudes. That's how we're salt and light for Jesus. When we put others before ourselves, we're showing God's love. When we take time to help someone**

YOU'LL NEED:

✓ **Bible**
✓ ***Grow Together Now* DVD**
✓ **DVD player**

or be a good friend, we're showing God's love. When people watch our actions, they should be able to see God's love shining in everything we do.

LIGHT FORCE

Give each child a small paper plate and a marker. Ask each person to draw a simple candle on one side of each paper plate and to write his or her name below it. When everyone is finished, have kids place their plates candle-side down anywhere on the floor. Next, have kids stand by a wall while you and other leaders add extra blank plates to the ones on the floor.

Ask for a volunteer to be the first to join the "Light Force" and to stand in the center of the sea of plates.

Say: **I'm going to play some music as everyone begins walking around the room. The person who is part of the Light Force has an important job to do: That person must quickly turn over as many of the candles as possible before the music stops. However, that's not as easy as it sounds! While our Light Force member is uncovering candles, the rest of you will be covering them up by turning them back over. When the music stops, everybody freeze.**

When kids are ready, start the game.

Play a fun worship song as kids move around the room. Pause the music several times. Each time, read the names on the plates that are uncovered. Remove those plates, and invite those kids to join the Light Force. Anyone who is added to the Light Force will start uncovering candles rather than covering them. Play until all the kids are part of the Light Force. Congratulate them for helping spread the light.

Afterward, lead this discussion:

- **What does it look like when kids shine for Jesus?**

- **How was this game like the way we shine God's love in our world?**

- **What are ways kids your age sometimes hide their light? Explain.**

Say: **If you know Jesus, you can shine for him wherever you are—that's how** *we show God's kindness to the world.* **Shine his love to others everywhere you go and it will be contagious!**

ASK/ANSWER

Say: **One way** *we show God's kindness to the world* **is by helping people ask and find answers to questions they have about Jesus and the Bible. Let's practice that right now.**

Form groups, with up to three children in each group. (If yours is a smaller class, it's okay if there are only one or two groups.) Hand out a Bible, a 3x5 card, and a pencil to each group. Have kids designate one person in each group as the Reporter, one as the Reader, and one as the Speaker.

First, instruct the Readers in each group to read aloud Matthew 5:13-16 to the others in their groups, and tell everyone else to begin thinking of good questions to ask about what they are hearing. (It's okay if the Reader reads the passage more than once!) Next, have groups talk about any questions they have that come to mind about Matthew 5:13-16. Tell the Reporters to write down their groups' three best questions.

Finally, allow time for the Speakers in each group to share one or two of their questions with the whole class.

Afterward, say: **Those are some great questions! You all are deep thinkers!**

Ask kids to discuss the following in their small groups:

- **Why is it important for us to ask questions that help us understand the Bible?**

- **What do you do when others ask you questions about the Bible?**

Say: **Helping your friends and family find answers to questions about the Bible is one fantastic way** *we show God's kindness to the world.* **Now that you've had practice at it, try it at home this week!**

✓ **Bibles**
✓ **3x5 cards**
✓ **pencils**

SIT/STAND

Say: **Matthew 5:16 tells us to "let your good deeds shine out for all to see, so that everyone will praise your heavenly Father." What that means is** *we show God's kindness to the world* **by our attitudes and by the things we do. Let's explore this a little more through a game called "Sit/Stand."**

Explain to kids that you are going to announce certain "great deeds." If that deed is something they can do, they should stand up. If they can't do it, they should sit down. Read a few "deeds" from this list, or make up your own by mixing "impossible" tasks with acts of kindness:

- **Fly to the moon and have a picnic.**
- **Help make lunch for someone in your family.**
- **Build a brand-new car using only toothpicks and a golf club.**
- **Ride along to keep your parents company when they go on errands.**
- **Sell 100,000 tickets for a stadium rock concert featuring a person who doesn't sing.**
- **Invite a friend to join you in singing a worship song.**
- **Graduate from college tomorrow.**
- **Help a friend with homework.**
- **Get a million people to watch a video of you blowing hair out of your eyes.**
- **Make a treat for a neighbor.**
- **Sweep the dust out of the Grand Canyon.**
- **Cheerfully help out with chores around the house.**
- **Work a miracle with your bare hands.**
- **Pray for your family and friends.**

Say: **There are a lot of things we can't do in life, but one thing everyone can do is be kind. When we are kind to others,** *we show God's kindness to the world.*

✓ **washable markers**

LIVE IT!

Say: **In Matthew 5:14, Jesus compared us to "light of the world." Let's have a little artistic fun as a way to remind us to be God's light and to shine his kindness in our world.**

Have kids form pairs, and give each pair a washable marker.

Say: **Draw a candle flame on your partner's pointer finger. The flame of the candle should be drawn on the fingernail and tip of the finger. Be careful and do a good job—but don't worry! Since we're using washable markers, you'll be able to wash the drawing off with soap and water after class.**

Give kids a moment to draw the finger-candles, and then invite everyone to wave their "candles" in the air.

Say: **When Jesus tells us to be salt and light, it means he wants us to live in a way that causes people to want to know God. Like candles shining in the darkness, when *we show God's kindness to the world*, people see God's love reflected through us.**

If time allows, lead kids in singing "This Little Light of Mine," and encourage them to create hand motions using their "finger candles" to go along with the song. Finish with a prayer asking Jesus to help us all show his kindness to the world.

TAKE-HOME PAGE

Give each child a Take-Home page. Encourage kids to select one of the six challenges for the week ahead.

PRACTICE KINDNESS

Keep growing in your faith and character. Choose one of the following challenges to do this week.

CHALLENGE 1

Each time you turn on a light today, think of a way to be a light for Jesus. Then do it!

CHALLENGE 2

This evening when it gets dark, walk through your house with a flashlight. In each room, pray that you'll light up the world like the flashlight lit up the room.

CHALLENGE 3

Be on the lookout for someone who is struggling today. Using your words or actions, find a way to show him or her God's love.

CHALLENGE 4

Think of one person you want to show God's love to—maybe someone you haven't always gotten along with or someone who seems lonely. Then think of one specific way to show that person God's love, and do it.

CHALLENGE 5

Look for the effects of light around you, such as things that have faded, a solar calculator working, or a parked car that's warmer inside because of the sun. When you see how light has changed the world around you, pray that you can shine's God light to change the world around you, too.

CHALLENGE 6

Every day for a week, pray, "God, help me be your light and show your kindness to the world—today!" Write down any experiences you have that you think might be God answering your prayer!

WE CAN GET ALONG WITH OTHERS

LEADER PREP

2 Samuel 15

LESSON AT A GLANCE

David and Absalom couldn't get along. David was king, but Absalom—David's son—wanted to be. And instead of waiting his turn and cooperating with his father in the meantime, Absalom made plans to take the throne for himself. David trusted God to work the situation out, and he eventually returned to the throne in Jerusalem. But his relationship with Absalom was never restored. Use this lesson to help children keep their relationships strong by getting along with others.

COOPERATION IS...
working together to accomplish a goal.

WHAT KIDS DO	WHAT YOU'LL NEED
God Sightings *(5 minutes)* Talk about ways they've seen God at work.	
Explore the Bible! *(10 minutes)* Watch a video about a bully, and discover that Jesus can help us all get along.	• Bible • *Grow Together Now* DVD • DVD player
Wanted: Crime Lab Artist *(15 minutes)* Sketch pictures of Absalom, and talk about consequences of conflict.	• Bible • paper • colored chalk
Give It a Shot *(10 minutes)* Cooperate to shoot baskets, and discuss ways to get better at cooperation.	• foam balls • several empty trash cans *(no lids)* • timer *(such as on a watch or cellphone)*
S.A.D. Sacks *(10 minutes)* Make hand puppets to help remember a strategy for living out Jesus' advice.	• Bible • 1 paper lunch bag per child • markers
Live It! *(15 minutes)* Try a challenge-experiment, and explore what it means to think of others first.	• bag of small, individually wrapped candies • marbles • golf ball • jar *(to hold the marbles and golf ball)*

ILLUSTRATED BY PAMELA JOHNSON

*Photocopy the Take-Home page at the end of this lesson for each child.

DEVOTIONS FOR LEADERS:

COOPERATION

Be aware of those around you today—including those you don't necessarily like. When you interact with them, listen for God's quiet voice whispering to you. What might God be saying about getting along with those who irritate you? who are rude to you? who use you? Then commit yourself to following through on what God is telling you, and do your part in getting along with those people.

BIBLE BACKGROUND FOR LEADERS

2 Samuel 15: Absalom Rebels

WHAT THE BIBLE SAYS

Absalom, the son of King David, wanted to replace his father on the throne. He worked hard to build up a following among the people, and he persuaded one of David's closest counselors to join him. When King David heard about the rebellion his son planned, he gathered his household and fled, knowing Absalom would come to Jerusalem and take the throne by force if necessary. The king chose to trust God. "If I find favor in the Lord's eyes," David said, "he will bring me back" (2 Samuel 15:25, NIV). When he was out of Jerusalem, David sent men to Absalom's court so they could pass information to David. One of the men, Hushai, was a trusted royal counselor. Hushai stayed in Jerusalem to offer advice to Absalom—advice designed to frustrate Absalom's plans.

WHAT IT MEANS

Absalom was ambitious and charismatic. Unfortunately, he used those qualities to subvert the rightful, God-anointed king. David could've stayed in Jerusalem and fought to retain his throne, but his leaving prevented the destruction of the city and the loss of lives—at least for the time being. There could be no peace in Israel while the throne was disputed. But eventually David mustered forces loyal to him and defeated Absalom in a costly battle (see 2 Samuel 18).

WHY IT MATTERS

Getting along with family members, co-workers, classmates, and others can be hard. Absalom's rebellion is an example of what not

ILLUSTRATED BY RONNIE ROONEY

to do. Most of us can relate to the reality of conflicts that could often be resolved with communication and compromise. As with David, we often don't know how those situations will turn out. But we can learn from David's example and entrust them to God.

THE LESSON

GOD SIGHTINGS

Use the text below or substitute your own examples for this weekly lesson-starter activity.

Say: **James 1:17 in the Bible reminds us that "Whatever is good and perfect is a gift coming down to us from God our Father." That means the gift of a beautiful sunset is evidence of God. When your friend shares with you, that's God's kindness at work. When you smile at others or hold open a door, you're showing God's joy.**

It's important that we recognize and thank God for the ways we see him all around us and the ways he is at work in our lives. We call these God Sightings.

Ask: **How have you seen God at work this week? What evidence have you seen of God's creativity, joy, forgiveness, and goodness?**

Think about God's creation, ways people have encouraged you, and even ways God helped you make a difference for someone else.

As a group, share God Sightings—ways you've each seen God at work. Then celebrate God's gifts in your lives with a prayer of thanksgiving.

EXPLORE THE BIBLE!

Summarize for kids the history of Absalom's rebellion against David, as recorded in 2 Samuel 15. Then say: **Sometimes we act like Absalom did. We don't always treat others nicely and get along with them. Today we have a video about a girl who didn't get along with others. The first part of the video**

YOU'LL NEED:

✓ **Bible**

✓ **Grow Together Now DVD**

✓ **DVD player**

is kind of sad, but watch for the way Jesus' love gives it a happy ending.

Play "Sarah's Story" (track 8) from the *Grow Together Now* DVD.

Afterward, lead this discussion:

- **What surprised you as you watched this video?**
- **If Sarah had been asked to help Absalom, what do you think she'd have told him?**
- **What do you think Sarah would tell you and me today about getting along with others?**

Say: **Absalom failed to get along with David, and it caused a war! Sarah learned to get along with others, and that made her friends with almost everyone in her school. Absalom shows us what not to do; Sarah shows us that, with God's help,** *we can get along with others.*

WANTED: CRIME LAB ARTIST

Give each child paper and a piece of chalk. Say: **You're the new Crime Lab Art Department of Ancient Israel. Your job is to sketch the notorious criminal Absalom. First I'll read his story in the Bible, and then I'll give you instructions for what to draw.**

Read aloud or summarize 2 Samuel 15 for kids.

Then say: **Absalom was handsome and strong, and he had long hair. Sketch a very quick, very rough picture of his head. Be sure to make him handsome!** Pause for kids to draw.

Say: **Here's more: Absalom was King David's son and wanted to be king himself. So he found men to help him take over his father's kingdom. That was sneaky and dangerous. Give Absalom's sneaky eyes in your drawing.** Pause. **King David heard what was happening, so he and some of his loyal followers ran away. That made Absalom happy, so draw a smile on that handsome, sneaky face.** Pause for kids to draw. Then ask them to share their drawings with each other.

YOU'LL NEED:

✓ **Bible**

✓ **paper**

✓ **colored chalk**

Say: **That wasn't easy! I kept changing what I wanted, didn't I? First I said to make Absalom handsome, then sneaky, and then happy. That's kind of the way Absalom was, though—a little shifty. He couldn't get along with his dad, so he spent four years sneaking around, getting people to like him so he could take over David's kingdom.**

Lead this discussion:

- **Absalom couldn't get along with his dad, so he planned to start a war. What do you think of that?**

- **What could Absalom and David have done to try to get along with each other?**

- **When Absalom and David couldn't get along, the whole kingdom suffered. Who gets hurt when you and I don't get along with others? Explain.**

Say: **Imagine how much better it would have been for both Absalom and David—and the whole kingdom!—if those two guys had just been able to get along. Someone should have told them that** *we can get along with others* **even if we don't like them.**

GIVE IT A SHOT

Remind kids of Absalom's rebellion against David, and say: **Can you imagine what Absalom and David might have accomplished if they'd worked together instead of working against each other? When** *we can get along with others,* **surprising things happen. Let's play a game to help us discover more about that.**

Have kids choose partners to form teams made up of two people. Set up several empty trash cans (no lids) around the room. Give each team one foam ball, and place the teams about 6 to 10 feet away from a trash can.

Advise kids that the trash can is the "basket" and the foam ball is their "basketball." The goal is to work as a team to shoot as many baskets as possible within 30 seconds, but each team member must have one hand on the ball when it is shot toward the trash can. Encourage kids to find ways to work together to make a lot of baskets as a team; then set your timer and let kids play.

YOU'LL NEED:

✓ **foam balls**
✓ **several empty trash cans (no lids)**
✓ **timer (such as on a watch or cellphone)**

After 30 seconds, pause the game and ask:

- **What are you learning that will help you improve at this game?**

Reset the timer and play another 30-second round. If time allows, repeat the question and play one last round before bringing all kids into a circle for discussion.

Ask:

- **What surprised you about this game?**

- **What did you do to get better at cooperating with your teammate?**

- **Getting along with others can sometimes feel hard. What can we do to get better at cooperating with others?**

Say: **Just as surprising things happened in his game, when *we can get along with others*, surprising things can happen in real life!**

S.A.D. SACKS

Say: **When I read about Absalom and David in the Bible, I wish they'd known what Jesus said in Matthew 7:12: "Do to others whatever you would like them to do to you." If they'd followed that advice, they could have avoided a lot of pain and trouble!**

Ask: **Why do you think it's hard sometimes for us to follow Jesus' advice to "Do to others whatever you would like them to do to you"?**

Say: **Let's do ourselves a favor now and make a craft to help us follow Jesus' advice, even when it seems hard.**

Give every child a paper bag and a marker. Instruct kids to use their supplies to make a sack puppet—one that will remind them to "Stop-Ask-Do" next time they're tempted not to get along with someone.

Have kids draw a silly "face" on the flap side of the paper sack, where the bottom fold of the sack becomes the mouth. Next, have kids write "Stop!" on one side of the sack, "Ask," on another side,

The easiest way to team-shoot a basket is for one partner to place a left hand on the ball and the other partner to place a right hand on the ball, then for both partners to shoot that ball at the same time. Still, give kids a few minutes to see if they can figure that out for themselves before cluing them in to that strategy.

YOU'LL NEED:

✓ **Bible**
✓ **1 paper lunch bag per child**
✓ **markers**

and "Do" on the back. Encourage kids to be creative and have fun as they decorate their sack puppets.

When everyone is ready, have kids put their sack puppets on their hands.

Say: **When you're tempted not to get along with someone, let your sack puppet help you. First, "Stop!"** (have kids hold up that side of their puppets) **and try to calm yourself down a bit. Next "Ask"** (have kids hold out that side of their puppets) **yourself "What would I want someone else to do for me in this situation?" Then "Do"** (have kids display the back of their puppets for their friends) **to that other person whatever you wish they would do for you. Stop-Ask-Do!** *We can get along with others* **better when we remember to Stop, Ask, and Do.**

LIVE IT!

Say: *We can get along with others* **when we learn how to think of others instead of thinking only of ourselves. Let's see what that looks like.**

Place the candy where kids can see it. Hold up the jar with the golf ball and the marbles inside. Say: **I'm going to reach my hand into this jar and remove the golf ball. How many of you think I can do it?** Pause; then attempt to remove the ball by wrapping it in your palm. Doing that will make your fist too big to fit out of the jar opening. When you can't remove the golf ball, say: **My hands are pretty big. Do any of you think you can do it?**

Continue: **Let's try a challenge-experiment. If you can wrap the ball in the palm of your hand and take it out of the jar without letting go, you get to keep this entire bag of candy all for yourself. However, if you choose instead to grab a marble, I'll give you enough candy so that everyone can have one piece. You only get one turn to try, so decide which item you want to go for!**

Have each child attempt to remove either the ball or a marble. Encourage kids to cheer for each other as they attempt this challenge. Award candy to all kids who remove a marble. Afterward, have kids share so that no child is left out of getting candy.

YOU'LL NEED:

✓ **bag of small, individually wrapped candies**

✓ **marbles**

✓ **golf ball**

✓ **jar (to hold the marbles and golf ball)**

FOR LEADERS:

When kids make a fist to hold the golf ball, that should make the child's hand too big to fit back through the jar opening. Still, it's best to practice this ahead of time just to make sure the opening of your jar isn't too big.

Lead this discussion:

- **What did you learn from this activity?**

- **In this experiment, everyone got candy when we all thought of others. In real life, what happens when we try to think of others and not just of ourselves?**

- **What's one thing you could do this week to help you get better at thinking of others?**

Say: **When we learn to put other people first, *we can get along with others* and everyone wins!**

TAKE-HOME PAGE

Give each child a Take-Home page. Encourage kids to select one of the six challenges for the week ahead.

PRACTICE COOPERATION

Keep growing in your faith and character. Choose one of the following challenges to do this week.

CHALLENGE 1

At least one time each day for a week, practice the "Stop-Ask-Do" strategy of getting along with others. First, "Stop!" and try to calm yourself down a bit. Next "Ask" yourself "What would I want someone else to do for me in this situation?" Then "Do" to another person whatever you wish they would do for you. Stop, Ask, Do!

CHALLENGE 2

Read Matthew 7:12, and brainstorm ideas for what it means to live out that verse today.

CHALLENGE 3

Ask three people the following question: "What's the best advice you have for getting along with others?"

CHALLENGE 4

Think of someone you're currently having a hard time getting along with. Pray that God would show you how to get along with that person better. Listen to what God has to say, and then look for opportunities to live out what he tells you.

CHALLENGE 5

Read Proverbs 15:1, and look for opportunities to live out that verse today.

CHALLENGE 6

Every day for a week, pray, "God, show me how you can help me get along with others." Write down any experiences you have that you think might be God answering your prayer!

LESSON 10 | WE CAN GET ALONG WITH OTHERS

GOD GIVES US GIFTS TO SERVE OTHERS

LEADER PREP

Acts 6:1-7

LESSON AT A GLANCE

In the days of the early church, some Christians needed help making sure people in their group were getting enough food. The apostles met together and decided to ask seven men to serve the church and use their gifts to solve this problem. God gave the seven men gifts to help others, and he gives us specific gifts to help others, too! Use this lesson to help children learn that just like these men used their gifts to help others, they can do the same!

COOPERATION IS...
working together to accomplish a goal.

WHAT KIDS DO	WHAT YOU'LL NEED
God Sightings *(5 minutes)* Talk about ways they've seen God at work.	
Explore the Bible! *(10 minutes)* Act out and discuss verse by verse Acts 6:1-7.	• Bible
Lunch Service *(15 minutes)* Watch a video of kids serving others, and explore how they can serve others too.	• *Grow Together Now* DVD • DVD player
Many Legs *(10 minutes)* Compete in a race, and discuss how they can work together to serve.	• duct tape • scissors *(to cut lengths of duct tape)* • stopwatch or timer
Hat Trick *(10 minutes)* Help each other discover how to use their gifts to serve others.	• fun hat
Live It! *(15 minutes)* Make hand-tracings, and encourage each other about God's gifts.	• paper • washable markers

*Photocopy the Take-Home page at the end of this lesson for each child.

ILLUSTRATED BY RONNIE ROONEY

DEVOTIONS FOR LEADERS:

COOPERATION

What talents has the Holy Spirit developed in you? Are you using them to serve God? God gave you gifts to uniquely equip you to serve others and the church. If you're using your talents to the full potential, great! If not, pray today that you'll be able to use your gifts in a way that expands and serves God's family!

BIBLE BACKGROUND FOR LEADERS

Acts 6:1-7: Seven Men Are Chosen to Serve

TENSION ARISES

Today's passage opens with a dispute between two groups: the Greek-speaking Christians and the Hebrew-speaking Christians. While both groups were probably Jewish, it's likely that they were unable to speak each other's languages, which probably added to the tension. It's also believed that there were Gentile converts to Judaism among the Greek Christians, which could've brought out some feelings of resentment and prejudice from the Hebrew-speaking Jews.

SERVING THE POOR

It was a tradition during this time to care for the poor and widowed by distributing food and other supplies. The disciples seemed to be in charge of this practice and involved in the distribution themselves. The Greek Christians began to complain that their widows weren't getting enough food, which may've been an accidental oversight on the part of the Hebrew-speaking Christians or an intentional act of prejudice. Either way, it immediately began to cause tension between the two groups.

SOLVING A PROBLEM

The apostles knew that this division would be extremely detrimental to the church, so they got together to make a plan. They felt that, although the distribution of food was a worthy cause, it wasn't the best use of their gifts for the disciples themselves to be in charge of that project. So they decided that the whole group of believers should choose seven men to continue to minister to the church in this way, while the apostles would devote their time to prayer and preaching.

SPECIAL TALENTS

It's important to realize that each of the seven chosen men was picked because he had unique talents that would allow him to carry on with the distribution of supplies and to make sure it was done fairly. Paul described Stephen as being "full of faith and the Holy Spirit." Because of these men's willingness to use their talents to serve, the church flourished and many new people believed in God.

THE LESSON

GOD SIGHTINGS

Use the text below or substitute your own examples for this weekly lesson-starter activity.

Say: **James 1:17 in the Bible reminds us that "Whatever is good and perfect is a gift coming down to us from God our Father." That means the gift of a beautiful sunset is evidence of God. When your friend shares with you, that's God's kindness at work. When you smile at others or hold open a door, you're showing God's joy.**

It's important that we recognize and thank God for the ways we see him all around us and the ways he is at work in our lives. We call these God Sightings.

Ask: **How have you seen God at work this week? What evidence have you seen of God's creativity, joy, forgiveness, and goodness?**

Think about God's creation, ways people have encouraged you, and even ways God helped you make a difference for someone else.

As a group, share God Sightings—ways you've each seen God at work. Then celebrate God's gifts in your lives with a prayer of thanksgiving.

EXPLORE THE BIBLE!

Form two groups. Tell Group A that they are going to be the Actors and Group B that they will be the Teachers.

Say: **I'm going to read about something that happened during the time the church first began. Actors, your job is to act out what happened. Teachers, your job will be to help us decide what we learn from the story. Ready? Here we go.**

Read aloud Act 6:1-7, one verse at a time. For each verse, invite one or two volunteers from each group to join you up front. Ask the Actors to act out the scene while you read the verse. After reading each verse, ask the Teachers to brainstorm one or two ideas of what the class might learn from the verse they've just seen and heard.

Afterward, have everyone applaud for both Actors and Teachers, and then ask:

- **If we boiled everything down to one idea, what would you say is the most important thing we can learn from this event in the Bible?**

- **Why do you think the disciples cared whether or not some people got food?**

- **What do you think would've happened if the men who were chosen had refused to serve food to the widows?**

Say: **We can learn many things from Acts 6:1-7, but one important thing it teaches us is that** *God gives us gifts to serve others.*

LUNCH SERVICE

Say: **Acts 6:1-7 even tells about a time when several of Jesus' followers were chosen for special service: To feed others! They aren't the only ones who've done that. Let's watch a video that'll show you what I mean.**

Show "Lunch Service" (track 9) from the *Grow Together Now* DVD.

Afterward ask:

- **What's going through your mind after seeing the kids in this video?**

- **How can you use your gifts to serve others?**

- **Tell about a time you served someone. What was that like?** Tell an example from your own life; then let kids share.

Say: **You might be good at sports, at music, or even at telling jokes. No matter what your talent is, you can use it to do things for other people. We don't have to be selfish with our talents because** *God gives us gifts to serve others.*

MANY LEGS

Invite kids to compete in this version of the classic "three-legged race." Have everyone choose a partner to form teams of two. Have each pair stand side by side and use duct tape to bind their two inside legs together. Have each team take a turn racing in tandem with arms around each other's shoulders, from a starting line to a finish line.

Time each team to see which is the fastest. Also award "bonus points" for teams that exhibit "Best Cooperation," "Best Attitude," "Most Fun to Watch," and "Most Likely to Need Crutches Before Age 21."

Afterward, ask:

- **What did you learn from this race about working together?**

- **What made it harder to work together? And what made it easier?**

Say: **We can accomplish great things when we work together. In fact, Acts 6:1-7 tells about how Jesus' friends worked together to serve others and make sure everyone was fed.** *That* **was such a big deal that it was included in the Bible!**

Ask:

- **What are ways** *we* **can work together to serve others? Let's brainstorm ideas.**

Say: **Those are great ideas, and they remind us that** *God gives us gifts to serve others.* **We all have special gifts we can use to team up in acts of service.**

HAT TRICK

Have everyone sit in a circle. Say: *God gives us gifts to serve others.* **Jesus' followers discovered that firsthand when they learned how to serve food so that everyone had enough.**

Tell kids that God has given each of them gifts too, but that sometimes it may be hard to know how to use those gifts. That's why you are all going to help each other with this next activity.

Show kids a fun hat. Tell them you're going to give the hat to someone in the circle, and the person receiving it must wear the hat while answering this question: "What's one thing you are good at doing?" After the person responds, others in the circle must take turns answering the question, "How can this person use that ability to serve others?" Allow two or three kids to brainstorm answers; then pass the hat to someone new and repeat. Keep going as long as time allows or until everyone has had a turn.

Say: **God doesn't make mistakes, and he's made sure that each and every one of us is gifted at** *something.* **Once we figure out what that is, we can start experimenting with ideas for how to use that gift because** *God gives us gifts to serve others.*

LIVE IT!

Have kids each trace a hand onto a piece of paper using washable markers. Then instruct kids to switch tracings with a partner.

Say: **Think about personality gifts that God has given your partner, such as friendliness, math skills, a cheerful attitude, or a good memory for the Bible. Write down or draw symbols for five cool qualities you see in your partner—one on each finger of the tracing.**

Give kids time to write or draw their ideas, and then have partners switch back so they have their own hand-tracing again. Have kids explain to each other what they wrote or drew. Then have kids

place their hand-tracings over their hearts as you pray, asking God to help them use their gifts to serve others.

Say: **Each one of you has great personality gifts from God! This week try to remember that** *God gives us gifts to serve others.*

TAKE-HOME PAGE

Give each child a Take-Home page. Encourage kids to select one of the six challenges for the week ahead.

PRACTICE COOPERATION

Keep growing in your faith and character. Choose one of the following challenges to do this week.

CHALLENGE 1

Ask your pastor, parent, or Sunday school teacher to help you figure out what gifts God has given you. Think of how you can use those gifts to serve others.

CHALLENGE 2

Ask a family member to look through the news on a reputable website or watch the news with you to find examples of people serving others. Talk about how you can use your gifts to serve others.

CHALLENGE 3

Wrap a box with a hole in the top. Write friends' gifts on paper and put them in the box. Then share with your friends what you wrote and talk about how the gifts can be used to serve God.

CHALLENGE 4

Take a walk with a friend and observe the people you see. As you walk, talk about all the ways you see people using their gifts to serve others. On your way home, brainstorm ideas for ways you and your friend could help others.

CHALLENGE 5

Hang a gift tag on your bathroom mirror. Whenever you see the tag, remember to thank God for the gifts he has given you. Ask God for help in using those gifts to serve others.

CHALLENGE 6

Every day for a week, pray, "God, thank for you the gifts you've given me. Please show me how to use my gifts to serve others." Write down any experiences you have that you think might be God answering your prayer!

WE WORK TO GET ALONG WITH OUR FAMILIES

LEADER PREP

Genesis 13:1-18

LESSON AT A GLANCE

Abram and Lot had a conflict because they could no longer support both of their families' flocks and herds living together. In this culture, etiquette dictated that Lot allow Abram to take whatever he wanted since he was older. But Abram was willing to give up what was rightfully his to keep peace within his family. Use this lesson to help kids learn to work to get along with their families.

COOPERATION IS...
working together to accomplish a goal.

WHAT KIDS DO	WHAT YOU'LL NEED
God Sightings *(5 minutes)* Talk about ways they've seen God at work.	
Explore the Bible! *(10 minutes)* Form a moving huddle, and discuss family relationships.	• Bible
Snack Attack *(15 minutes)* Feed each other a snack, and talk about family cooperation.	• pretzel sticks • marshmallows • table • paper towels • blindfolds • hand sanitizer
Up in the Air *(10 minutes)* Play a musical game, and discover how important each person is within a family.	• foam balls, tennis balls, and/or small sports balls—enough for every child to have 1 • upbeat worship music
Prayer Practice *(10 minutes)* Practice praying for people in their families.	• 3 poster boards • markers • masking tape
Live It! *(15 minutes)* Create "I Can Help" coupons to share with members of their families.	• colorful paper • pencils or markers

*Photocopy the Take-Home page at the end of this lesson for each child.

ILLUSTRATED BY PAMELA JOHNSON

DEVOTIONS FOR LEADERS:

COOPERATION

When it comes to family, it can be hard to give up what we see as our rights and "lay down our lives" for our family members. We say to ourselves, "This won't change anything," "They'll just keep taking advantage of the situation," or "Am I really helping them by doing this?" But God doesn't ask us to make excuses—God asks us to work to get along with our families. This week, spend a few moments talking to God about a relationship in your family that you're struggling with. Open your heart to hear how God wants you to reach out in forgiveness and acceptance to that person, and work to get along with him or her, no matter what the past has been like.

BIBLE BACKGROUND FOR LEADERS

Genesis 13:1-18: Abram Is Generous to Lot

FAMILY CONFLICT

Abram and Lot had gone south into Egypt because of a famine in the land of Canaan. While in Egypt, Abram became a very wealthy man. When Pharaoh sent Abram away, Abram and Lot headed back to the land God had promised to Abram's descendants. In Genesis 13:5, we discover that Lot was wealthy as well. Yet it became apparent that Lot and Abram could no longer support both of their families' flocks and herds living together. Conflicts between their herdsmen over land use could have easily become quarrels between Abram and Lot.

KEEPING THE PEACE

In this situation and culture, etiquette dictated that Lot allow Abram to take whatever he deemed was rightfully his because Abram was the respected elder and also more powerful and wealthy. Younger people cared for and respected elder family members. So Abram's offer probably shocked Lot—this was turning out far better than he had hoped! He had fully expected to end up with the harshest, least fertile part of the land, but here was his chance to keep the fertile valley. Abram was willing to give up what was rightfully his to keep peace within his family. Lot, thinking only of himself, made a choice that his entire culture would have deemed unthinkable—he kept the good land

ILLUSTRATED BY RONNIE ROONEY

for himself. The actions of these two men demonstrated the differences in their hearts.

A BLESSING

Sometimes the selfishness of other people in our families makes getting along with them hard work. It's very important that we strive to maintain healthy, harmonious relationships with the family God has given us. We need to be sure we don't contribute to any strife by our own actions. Just as God blessed Abram for working to get along with Lot, God will bless you for working to get along with your own family members!

THE LESSON

GOD SIGHTINGS

Use the text below or substitute your own examples for this weekly lesson-starter activity.

Say: **James 1:17 in the Bible reminds us that "Whatever is good and perfect is a gift coming down to us from God our Father." That means the gift of a beautiful sunset is evidence of God. When your friend shares with you, that's God's kindness at work. When you smile at others or hold open a door, you're showing God's joy.**

It's important that we recognize and thank God for the ways we see him all around us and the ways he is at work in our lives. We call these God Sightings.

Ask: **How have you seen God at work this week? What evidence have you seen of God's creativity, joy, forgiveness, and goodness?**

Think about God's creation, ways people have encouraged you, and even ways God helped you make a difference for someone else.

As a group, share God Sightings—ways you've each seen God at work. Then celebrate God's gifts in your lives with a prayer of thanksgiving.

✓ **Bible**

EXPLORE THE BIBLE!

Say: **Let's start off by looking at a Bible passage about a guy named Abram and his nephew, Lot.**

Read aloud Genesis 13:1-18.

Then say: **Let's see if we can get a feel for what it might've been like for Abram and Lot at this time.** Have everyone stand and huddle together in a circle, back to back. Say: **God told Abram to pack up all his belongings and his family and travel to a new place. Abram and his nephew Lot had many sheep, goats, cattle, and other possessions. They formed a huge group as they set out on their journey.**

Have kids walk together across the room, staying huddled close together and overcoming any obstacles along the way together.

Say: **They settled near a town called Bethel, but the land wasn't big enough for everyone. Abram's herdsmen and Lot's herdsmen started to fight. Abram didn't want his family to fight, so he told Lot to choose which part of the land he wanted. Lot chose the best half of the land, and Abram took the rest.**

Have kids return to their seats. Then lead this discussion.

Say: **Family often has to live in a crowded space, and just like it was hard for us to maneuver in a crowded huddle, it can be hard for family members to get along in that crowded space. That can cause arguments and fights, like what happened with Abram and Lot.**

Ask:

• **How do you handle it when you have arguments and fights with people in your family?**

• **Abram settled his family argument by letting Lot choose the best land while he took second-best. Why do you think Abram did that?**

• **What advice do you think Abram might give us about getting along with our family members?**

Say: **Family was important to Abram, and he proved it when he gave Lot the best land—and brought peace to his relatives. He showed us that good things happen when** *we work to get along with our families.*

SNACK ATTACK

Say: **Let's try a little experiment now called "Snack Attack." If we're able to work together for this, we'll all get a great snack!**

Have kids choose a partner to form pairs. Designate one partner in each pair as the Eater and one as the Feeder. Pass around hand sanitizer so everyone has clean hands for this activity.

Invite pairs of kids to stand around a table you've set up in front, and set two pretzel sticks and two marshmallows on a paper towel in front of each pair. Have the Eater stand facing the table, with arms behind his or her back. Have the Feeder stand behind the Eater and loop hands underneath the Eater's arms so it looks as though the Feeder's arms are actually the Eater's arms.

Say: **The goal here is to help each other so everyone can get a tasty marshmallow and pretzel snack. Feeders, you must assemble the snack and place it—gently—in the Eater's mouth. Eaters, you must give the Feeder proper directions to help your partner succeed in getting you that snack. Oh, and by the way—Feeders, you'll be blindfolded!**

Blindfold the Feeders, and then let Feeders try to poke a pretzel into a marshmallow and feed it to the Eater. Next have kids switch roles and try again.

Afterward, have everyone quickly clean up any mess; then ask:

- **What were you thinking when you were the Eater? and when you were the Feeder?**

- **What ideas do you have about cooperation after doing this activity?**

- **How could those ideas help you become better at cooperating with your family at home?**

YOU'LL NEED:

✓ **pretzel sticks**
✓ **marshmallows**
✓ **table**
✓ **paper towels**
✓ **blindfolds**
✓ **hand sanitizer**

Say: **In Genesis 13, Abram and Lot learned that when *we work to get along with our families*, everyone benefits. We learned that with our "Snack Attack" experiment, too. So when you're at home this week, try to remember and practice being cooperative with others in your family.**

UP IN THE AIR

Say: **Sometimes it's hard to get along with our families. Our sisters or brothers annoy us, or we don't like our parents' rules. Let's see if we can picture what it's like when we don't get along with others in our families.**

Give each child a small ball for this game—foam balls work great, or use tennis balls, small sports balls, or some mixture of all three. Play upbeat worship music in the background. Then have everyone stand in a circle. Have kids toss the balls to the person on their right, being sure to keep the balls moving without dropping any.

After a minute, pick someone to step out of the circle, but leave his or her ball moving in the circle. Every minute or so, tell another person to step out of the circle, but don't take any of the balls out of the circle rotation. Stop the music when there are only two people left.

Lead this discussion:

- **What problems did it cause here when people stepped out of the circle?**

- **If you "stepped out" of your family and refused to get along with them, what problems might come up at home?**

- **What do you think is most helpful when you are struggling to get along with people in your family?**

Say: **When Abram and Lot were arguing, Abram refused to "step out" of family difficulties. Instead, Genesis 13:8 tells us that "Abram said to Lot, 'Let's not allow this conflict to come between us.' " We can have the same kind of helpful attitude in our homes today when *we work to get along with our families*.**

PRAYER PRACTICE

Before class, use poster board and markers to make three "Prayer Prompt" signs as follows:

YOU'LL NEED:

✓ **3 poster boards**

✓ **markers**

✓ **masking tape**

SIGN #1:

Pray for Your Parents

- their relationships with Jesus

- things they worry about

- their jobs and/or volunteer work

- anything else you'd like to pray about for them

SIGN #2:

Pray for Your Brother(s) and Sister(s)

- their relationships with Jesus

- things they worry about

- their school, jobs, and/or volunteer work

- anything else you'd like to pray about for them

SIGN #3:

Pray for Your Relatives (aunts, uncles, grandparents, cousins, and so on)

- their relationships with Jesus

- things they worry about

- their school, jobs, and/or volunteer work

- anything else you'd like to pray about for them

In class, use the masking tape to hang each Prayer Prompt sign on a wall of your room. Then say: *We work to get along with our families,* **and one of the best ways to do that is to pray for our family members every day. Sometimes that can feel hard, though. So today, let's spend a few minutes practicing what it might be like to pray for our families.**

Form three groups. Send Group 1 to stand in front of the first Prayer Prompt sign, Group 2 to the second sign, and Group 3 to the third sign. Say: **Quietly follow the instruction on your sign. Older kids, help younger kids read the signs, please.**

After a moment or two, have groups switch signs and repeat the process. Do this one more time, until every child has spent time praying in front of each sign. Gather kids in a circle.

Ask:

- **How does it feel to pray for people in our families?**

- **How can prayer help connect you to your family members?**

Say: **Prayer is one of the best ways *we work to get along with our families*. Let's do it often!**

LIVE IT!

Ask:

- **When each of us goes home this week, what are ways we might be helpful to others in our families? Let's brainstorm our best ideas.**

Give kids a chance to brainstorm, and then pass out colorful slips of paper and pencils (or markers) to each child. Give each child enough paper slips to match the number of people in his or her home.

Encourage kids to use their supplies and their brainstormed ideas to make one "I Can Help!" coupon for each person in their home. If there's time, suggest they include drawings on their coupons.

Give kids a few moments to work; then tell kids to deliver their coupons to family members this week.

Say: **Helping out others in our families is a really fun way that *we work to get along with our families*. People in your home are going to love it!**

Close your class time with prayer, thanking God for the many opportunities we have to cooperate with others in our families.

TAKE-HOME PAGE

Give each child a Take-Home page. Encourage kids to select one of the six challenges for the week ahead.

PRACTICE COOPERATION

Keep growing in your faith and character. Choose one of the following challenges to do this week.

CHALLENGE 1

Write out Genesis 13:8 by hand, and tape it to your bathroom mirror so you'll see it all week. Use it to follow Abram's example of valuing his family more than his circumstances.

CHALLENGE 2

Ask one of your parents to tell you about a time he or she had to work to get along with siblings or friends.

CHALLENGE 3

When you first wake up in the morning, pray for someone in your family.

CHALLENGE 4

Give generously to one of your siblings who wants something of yours today.

CHALLENGE 5

Ask God to show you anyone in your family who you need to get along with. If necessary, talk to the person and ask for forgiveness.

CHALLENGE 6

Every day for a week, pray, "God, show me how to get along better with people in my family—and help me do that work." Write down any experiences you have that you think might be God answering your prayer!

LESSON 12 | WE WORK TO GET ALONG WITH OUR FAMILIES

LEADER PREP

1 Corinthians 12:12-27

LESSON AT A GLANCE

Paul reminds us in 1 Corinthians that none of us is more important than anyone else and that we can all contribute to God's work, just as the parts of a body work together. Everyone is important and needed, just as the many different parts of our own bodies are needed. Use this lesson to help kids learn that when we work together as the body of Christ, God works through us.

COOPERATION IS...
working together to accomplish a goal.

WHAT KIDS DO	WHAT YOU'LL NEED
God Sightings *(5 minutes)* Talk about ways they've seen God at work.	
Explore the Bible! *(10 minutes)* Ask questions about 1 Corinthians 12:12-27, and attempt to put on shoes using elbows.	• Bible
Hand-Eye Coordination *(15 minutes)* Draw a portrait without seeing the model, and discover God's plan for cooperation.	• Bible • wig or silly hat • brightly colored coat or overshirt • silly prop *(such as a toy sword or superhero action figure)* • paper • colored pencils or markers
Rescue *(10 minutes)* Watch a video and see inspiring teamwork in action.	• Bible • *Grow Together Now* DVD • DVD player
Rainbow Reality *(10 minutes)* Draw a monochromatic rainbow, and then work together to create a many-colored one.	• paper • colored pencils *(enough for all kids to share)* • marker • craft paper *(white or brown)*
Live It! *(15 minutes)* Work together on a "Cool Idea" committee to create an exciting class service project.	• paper • pencils

ILLUSTRATED BY PAIGE BILLIN-FRYE

Photocopy the Take-Home page at the end of this lesson for each child.

DEVOTIONS FOR LEADERS:

COOPERATION

Today's passage shows us that God intended for the people in the church to work together. Every person in the church has a place and a purpose, so let's be open and ready to fill the position God has in mind for us. Kids are no exception; God has a plan for everyone. Look for ways even the smallest child can make a worthwhile contribution to the body of Christ.

BIBLE BACKGROUND FOR LEADERS

1 Corinthians 12:12-27: The Importance of Everyone

THE BODY OF CHRIST

In this passage, Paul explains to the Corinthians how the church is like a body—more specifically, the body of Christ. Apparently, some people in the early church felt insignificant, thinking their gifts to be less valuable (verses 14-20), while others felt overly important, thinking their gifts superior (verses 21-26). Paul lets Christians know that God has a purpose for everyone, no matter who they are or what kind of gifts they have.

EVERYONE HAS A PURPOSE

Paul's message is a great equalizer: People with gifts that may seem insignificant are actually much more important than they may think, and people with gifts that seem more spectacular aren't any more important than anyone else. "God has put each part just where he wants it" (verse 18). Even if you just have a paper cut on your finger, it can affect the whole body. A pain in one place means the rest of the body has to work harder. We all are part of that body, and God wants us to use the gifts he's given. When Christians work together, just like a human body, we can accomplish God's great plans.

ILLUSTRATED BY DANA REGAN

GOD SIGHTINGS

Use the text below or substitute your own examples for this weekly lesson-starter activity.

Say: **James 1:17 in the Bible reminds us that "Whatever is good and perfect is a gift coming down to us from God our Father." That means the gift of a beautiful sunset is evidence of God. When your friend shares with you, that's God's kindness at work. When you smile at others or hold open a door, you're showing God's joy.**

It's important that we recognize and thank God for the ways we see him all around us and the ways he is at work in our lives. We call these God Sightings.

Ask: **How have you seen God at work this week? What evidence have you seen of God's creativity, joy, forgiveness, and goodness?**

Think about God's creation, ways people have encouraged you, and even ways God helped you make a difference for someone else.

As a group, share God Sightings—ways you've each seen God at work. Then celebrate God's gifts in your lives with a prayer of thanksgiving.

EXPLORE THE BIBLE!

Say: **Believe it or not, the Bible says all of us who are Christians are like a body. That seems kind of strange, doesn't it? Let's hear what Paul meant when he wrote that.**

YOU'LL NEED:

✓ **Bible**

Read aloud 1 Corinthians 12:12-27. Then ask:

• **What questions do you have about what you just heard?**

Let kids ask a few questions, and if possible, let other kids try to answer the questions asked. Then say: **You and I are all like the parts of a body, and *when we work together, God can work***

YOU'LL NEED:

✓ **Bible**

✓ **wig or silly hat**

✓ **brightly colored coat or overshirt**

✓ **silly prop** (*such as a toy sword or superhero action figure*)

✓ **paper**

✓ **colored pencils or markers**

through us. **Let's try a little experiment to help us better understand that idea.**

Instruct everybody take off one shoe and place it nearby. Next, tell kids to put their shoes back on using only their elbows. Give kids a moment to try this, and then allow them to put their shoes on the traditional way.

Say: **Even for something as simple as putting on a shoe, a body needs *every* part working together to do its job. God's plan for us is for us to work together too.**

HAND-EYE COORDINATION

Say: **Here's a new challenge for you. Half of you are going to draw my portrait—sight unseen!**

Have kids choose a partner to form pairs, and designate one partner as the "Hand" and the other partner as the "Eye." Have pairs sit on the floor, facing each other in positions that require the Hand to have his or her back to you while the Eye sees you clearly. Distribute paper and colored pencils (or markers) to each Hand.

Say: **From now on, no Hand is allowed to turn around and look at me!**

Comically put on your costume: a wig or silly hat and a brightly colored coat or overshirt. Finish off your costume by happily brandishing a silly prop (such as a toy sword or superhero action figure).

Say: **All right, Eyes, describe to your partner what you see so that he or she can draw the finest portrait of me possible. Ready, go!**

Give kids a little time to work on their portraits. Afterward, allow a few teams to show off their work. Then have kids discuss these questions:

• **What went through your mind as you tried to create these portraits together?**

• **Were you surprised by how well you did? Explain why or why not.**

Say: **The simple fact is, no eye can draw without the hand, and no hand can draw without the eye. All parts of the body need each other—just like we all need each other. Listen to this:**

Read aloud 1 Corinthians 12:21, followed by 1 Corinthians 12:27.

Say: **God made us all unique, and because of that** *when we work together, God can work through us.*

RESCUE

Read 1 Corinthians 12:18, and then say: **We're like the parts of the body, and when we work as a team, great things happen! It's kind of like how a mountain search-and-rescue team works. Let's watch a video that'll show us more about that. For fun, see if you can count how many times the team members say "we" in this video.**

YOU'LL NEED:

✓ **Bible**

✓ *Grow Together Now* **DVD**

✓ **DVD player**

Show "Rescue!" (track 10) from the *Grow Together Now* DVD.

Afterward, lead this discussion:

- **These team members used the word "we" so many times! What do you think about that?**

- **What are the best examples of teamwork that you saw in this video?**

- **What do you think would happen if people like us imitated a search-and-rescue attitude in the way we acted at home or church? Describe it.**

Say: **Every person on a search-and-rescue team is so important. If they don't work together, they can't succeed. But when they cooperate well, they actually save people's lives! We may never be on search and rescue, but we can cooperate like them. As 1 Corinthians 12:18 reminds us,** *when we work together, God can work through us* **to do great things.**

YOU'LL NEED:

✓ **paper**
✓ **colored pencils**
   (enough for all kids to share)
✓ **marker**
✓ **craft paper**
   (white or brown)

FOR LEADERS

At the beginning of this activity, some kids may be tempted to swap pencils to add color to their individual drawings. Discourage this if you see it happening as you'll want to make the point that working alone yields only a monochromatic rainbow.

RAINBOW REALITY

Give each child a sheet of paper and one colored pencil. Say: **Working individually, use only your own pencil to draw a rainbow on your paper.**

Allow a moment for kids to draw; then ask for volunteers to show off their work.

Say: **Those are all finely drawn pictures, but...all of these rainbows have only one color in them. Rainbows are supposed to have many colors! What did you do wrong?** Invite kids to explain, and then say: **Yes, I think I see the problem too. We've been working individually when we could be working together. Let's start over.**

Spread a long sheet of craft paper (white or brown) on the floor, and invite children to create a large, colorful picture of a rainbow together. Encourage kids to work together, to share colors, and just to enjoy the creative moment.

While they're drawing the rainbow, use a marker to add the title *"When we work together, God can work through us"* to the drawing.

When everyone is finished, let kids stand back and admire their work. If possible, hang the rainbow on a wall of your room.

Ask:

• **What do you like best about this fantastic rainbow?**

• **How would you describe the difference between this rainbow and the one you made all by yourself?**

Say: **If we can create something this great just by working together for a short time, imagine what we could do in other areas!** Read aloud 1 Corinthians 12:12. Say: **God's plan really is best:** *When we work together, God can work through us.*

LIVE IT!

Say: **All day today I've been trying to teach you that** *when we work together, God can work through us.* **Now I want you to teach that truth to me. Here's how.**

Have kids form teams of up to four people. Tell kids that they are each now on a "Cool Idea Committee." Give each "committee" a sheet of paper and a pencil, and appoint one team member to take notes during the rest of this activity.

Say: **In the time we have left, I want your committee to brainstorm one really cool idea for a project that our class can do—something we can do together to serve people in our community. Think about it, talk about it, brainstorm, and find one great idea. Then think about all the things that would need to be done in order for us to pull off that idea. For instance, what supplies would we need? What specific things would people in our class need to do? How much time would it take? That kind of stuff. Be creative. Have fun. Go!**

Give kids as much time as possible to come up with their "really cool ideas." Then allow kids to briefly share their ideas with everyone. If possible, pick an idea and use it as a service project for your class!

Afterward, close this session with prayer, thanking Jesus for bringing us all together as one body, working together to do really cool things for him.

TAKE-HOME PAGE

Give each child a Take-Home page. Encourage kids to select one of the six challenges for the week ahead.

PRACTICE COOPERATION

Keep growing in your faith and character. Choose one of the following challenges to do this week.

CHALLENGE 1

Ask an adult to help you find a church directory or bulletin and explain to you what the different people listed do for your church. Choose one job you learned about. Create a list of things you could do to help the person with that job. At church on Sunday, look for the person you chose and offer your help.

CHALLENGE 2

Talk with a couple of friends about how you can work together to help someone else. Then do it as a team project— work together to choose a job for each person. Maybe you can help with yardwork, play with a little brother, or help a neighbor.

CHALLENGE 3

Draw four boxes on a piece of paper, and label the boxes "Eyes," "Ears," "Hands," and "Feet." Inside each box, write a brainstormed list of answers to this question: "How can I use this part of me to help others serve God?" For instance, you can use your eyes to read a book to children or your feet to run in a charity race. Try a few of your ideas this week!

CHALLENGE 4

Think about how your body works best when all parts are engaged. Time yourself doing simple tasks, such as making your bed or tying your shoes, with one arm behind your back. Then time yourself doing it with both arms. Ask God to help you be like his body, all working together to accomplish his goals.

CHALLENGE 5

Find an old towel, and pile several books onto the center of it. See how many books you can lift on your own. Now find a friend to help you, and see how many more books you can lift together. Tell your friend that when two people work together for God, it makes a task not only easier but more fun!

CHALLENGE 6

Every day for a week, pray, "God, show me how to work with others so you can work through all of us together." Write down any experiences you have that you think might be God answering your prayer!